What if Pigs Can Fly? *will help you look at curiosity differently. What I love the most about Van Lai-DuMone's approach to this is how PRACTICAL it is. She has a wonderful ability to take abstract concepts and make them real. Her use of storytelling, personal experiences, reflective exercises and an accompanying workbook, serve as a powerful way to drive her ideas home. This isn't a book that you'll read and forget. This is a book that will truly impact your life.*

—Leo Chan, Chief Innovation Igniter & Coach, Abound Innovation Inc.

What if Pigs Can Fly? *will inspire you to look at everyday moments with a new sense of wonder. It will reframe how you think about your own creative abilities and inspire you to bring curiosity into your professional and personal life. Van Lai-DuMone brings with her the unique ability to unearth the creative person in all of us. She leaves a lasting impression on the audiences that take her courses, listen to her talks or read her book. If you are looking for new tools to inspire your team and engage them so that information is received and retained, I highly recommend this book.*

—Jane Maine, CEO & Founder, Contenta Meetings & Events

What if Pigs Can Fly? *allows the reader to soar and live into one's dreams and passions by learning how to follow curiosity. The insights and strategies for living a life of wonder and wisdom are based on brain science and the author's insight and experience. The examples are inspiring, and the accompanying workbook is a great guide for achieving excellence one small step at a time. This book will elevate your creative spirit.*

—Robert Maurer, PhD, Author of *One Small Step Can Change Your Life: The Kaizen Way*

If creativity drives innovation, then it is curiosity that drives creativity. Therefore, developing your curiosity is a must, and Van Lai-DuMone shows you how to get there. This book lays out a clear and implementable method for increasing curiosity, which can be an abstract term for some. Lai-DuMone's style of interactive teaching is a breath of fresh air and really engages the learner to take ownership of their development. She's a great teacher and an even greater inspiration, through her powerful stories that drive this book. What if Pigs Can Fly? *is a must read if you wish to improve your creative thinking by strengthening your curiosity.*

—Genein Letford, M.Ed, Author of *7 Gems of Intercultural Creativity*®, Founder & CEO CAFFE Strategies, INC

What if Pigs Can Fly? *might just hold the key to unlocking your creative future. This book (and program) guided us to take those important first small steps we needed to launch our Playsonality© Playstyles Program. After applying the philosophy Lai-DuMone presents so simply, I was able to isolate that one small thing that was somehow blocking our progress. We have since successfully launched our program in multiple cities around the world. This inspirational and practical book is a reminder that we are all capable of achieving unlimited possibilities when we choose to consider, "What if Pigs Can Fly?"*

—Jacqueline Lloyd Smith, Author, Master Trainer in LEGO® SERIOUS PLAY® methods, Founder of Strategic Play Global

WHAT IF PIGS CAN FLY?

Curiosity is the most powerful thing we own. Follow yours!
- [illegible signature]

FOR: Defensive Tactics Camp Attendees Only

WHAT IF PIGS CAN FLY?

A PRACTICAL GUIDE
TO FOLLOW YOUR CURIOSITIES
TO ACHIEVE IMPRACTICAL POSSIBILITIES

VAN LAI-DUMONE

THIN LEAF PRESS | LOS ANGELES

Library of Congress Cataloging-in-Publication Data
Names: Author, Lai-DuMone, Van
Title: *What if Pigs Can Fly?* A Practical Framework to Follow Your Curiosities to Achieve Impractical Possibilities

LCCN 2023922939

ISBN 978-1-953183-43-9 (paperback) | 978-1-953183-42-2 (eBook)

Professional Development, Creativity

Editor: Erik Seversen
Illustrator: Sarah Moyle
Cover Design: 100 Covers
Interior Design: Formatted Books
Thin Leaf Press
Los Angeles

This is not a mission to the moon.

Yet following curiosity might be just as intimidating to you as navigating your way to the moon. That's why I wrote this book. To give you a simple framework that makes following your curiosity an attainable step-by-step process. You'll see for yourself that pigs *can* fly as you turn your wild curiosities into amazing possibilities!

Van

#whatifpigscanfly
worksmartadvantage.com/whatifpigscanfly
Watch my TEDx Talk, What If? The Life Changing Power of Curiosity and Courage

For my mom, who taught me that all things are possible.
And my dad, who now gets to fly again.

Cu·ri·os·i·ty

noun

A: inquisitive interest; desire to know

B: interest leading to inquiry

… and possibility!

CONTENTS

INTRODUCTION

(The book starts here. Don't skip this!)

My life moves at a fast pace, I'm pretty sure yours does too. We often find ourselves caught up in the hustle of "I have to," "I should," as well as juggling a laundry list of activities and to dos. With all that commotion, often bordering on chaos, it's not surprising that many of us have lost touch with our innate curiosity and sense of wonder that comes to us as whispers of ideas tapping us on the shoulder. I wrote *What If Pigs Can Fly?* to give you tools to pause long enough to hear those whispers and act on the ideas that come seeking your attention. In doing so, you'll be able to explore life from fresh perspectives and transform challenges into opportunities, to achieve even the most impractical possibilities. There is magic in curiosity. My hope is that you discover, or rather rediscover, yours through this book.

Inspired by a little polymer clay flying pig dangling off a piece of fishing string on the rear-view mirror of my trusty 1993 Toyota Tercel I drove in college, I often reflected on this playful question, and now the title of this book, *What If Pigs Can Fly?* I spent countless hours in that car on road trips with friends and commuting up and down the Pacific Coast Highway between Los Angeles where I grew up and UC Santa Barbara. That whimsical polymer clay pig always in my peripheral view, swaying back and forth, soaring against the backdrop of cityscapes, mountains, and ocean. I think the presence of that flying pig subconsciously encouraged me to believe that the seemingly impossible is indeed possible. And if that little clay pig could take flight, you and I have the capacity to achieve anything we can imagine.

The purpose of this book is to take you on a journey of rediscovering your curiosities in a practical way. It guides you to take action on those curiosities through a framework that will teach you to ask powerful questions and take small mighty steps toward new possibilities. Whether that be a major life change like a work transition, moving to a new country, starting a business, or simply picking up a new hobby—this framework will act as your ally, supporting and emboldening you to take those ideas that have been tapping you on the shoulder, waiting for you to pay attention and bring them into reality.

In her book *Big Magic*, Elizabeth Gilbert refers to ideas as having consciousness and will. These willful ideas fly around seeking human partners to bring them to life. I propose that these ideas often come to us in the form of curiosities. This book challenges you to pay attention then act on the curiosities that come your way. Because in those curiosities are the potential of new doors opening, expansive fields to explore, playgrounds to tumble around on, and oceans of opportunity for you to dive into.

"An idea spends an eternity swirling around us, searching for available and willing human partners. When an idea thinks it has found someone ... the idea will pay you a visit."

—Elizabeth Gilbert, *Big Magic*

My interest about the invaluable impact of curiosity originates from my childhood and my family's incredible and unpredictable experiences as Vietnamese refugees in the United States.

In 1975, 20 Vietnamese refugee women arrived with their families to Hope Village Refugee Integration Center in Weimar, California. There, they met Hollywood movie star Tippi Hedren who was a volunteer at the camp. Through a series of inquisitive questions and small steps triggered by a curiosity, this group of women pioneered what is now the 8.3-billion-dollar manicure industry in the United States. One of these women was my mom.

The secret to these women's unintended accomplishment was the inadvertent application of a simple framework that I have since extracted from listening to and sharing their story. It is the framework I now teach in corporate trainings and through speaking engagements to encourage, motivate, and supply people with tools needed to follow their curiosities. This is the framework I will share with you.

You will read more about my family's journey in the pages of this book because it is our experiences that taught me that curiosity is powerful, life changing, worth following, and the most powerful thing we own.

What If Pigs Can Fly? is organized into four parts, collectively designed to enable you to live a more curious life. In the first part, you will practice strengthening your curiosity muscle by learning to actively rekindle your sense of wonder. In part two, pick up the art of asking "what if" questions to tap into your imagination and generate innovative ideas to pursue your curiosity. Part three guides you through taking incremental strides toward your curiosity and exploring new opportunities as they arise, step by step. To close, in part four, you'll discover how to prioritize and cultivate a curiosity-driven life by adopting new mindsets and behaviors that create a playground to nurture your curiosity.

Speaking about playgrounds, the interactive design of this book aligns with the approach I take in my work as a Fractional Learning and Development Officer and founder of my consultancy—worksmart Advantage, integrating creative thinking, play, and hands-on activities as part of the learning process. A 2022 research study from the Safety Sciences Department at Indiana University of Pennsylvania called "The Impact of Active Learning Strategies on Retention and Outcomes in Safety Training," states that "training delivered through hands-on activities, gamification, and group discussion can result in greater knowledge retention, as active learners retained 93.5% of previously learned information compared to only 79% for passive learners." With that in mind, allow creativity to take you out of your head and into your hands. As you read this book get out your paper, your pen, even colorful markers or crayons and work through the exercises.

Getting creative will engage you as an active participant in your learning, which allows for more insights to arise, stimulates the retention of the information you are presented with, and is undeniably more fun!

In addition to the creative activities, I will share anecdotes from my work throughout the book to illustrate how both curiosity and creativity have played valuable roles in my life and my career. Overall, I wrote this book in a way that gets you to activate your creativity and make curiosity a habit, challenges you, and moves you beyond your comfort zone. I do this because it's beyond our comfort zone that pigs *can* fly!

I have included the accompanying workbook in the back of this book. You can also download a copy at www.worksmartadvantage.com/whatifpigscanfly.

Why Creativity?

I'm often asked why I use creativity in my work. Here is a short list of my whys:

- Creativity is a capacity we all have. When we utilize creativity as a learning methodology, we tap into a resource that is unlimited in each of us.
- Creativity encourages us to use our imagination to see things from different perspectives.
- Creativity allows us to play and get out of our ego for unconscious ideas to arise.
- Creativity has the capacity to transform challenges into opportunities!

This book has the potential to inspire and empower you, encouraging you to embrace and utilize your innate creativity and curiosity. It aims to embolden you to take small steps toward achieving your big dreams. I'm excited that you've joined me on this amazing and magical journey as we explore together what it truly means to ask, 'What if pigs *can* fly?".

The Follow Your Curiosity Framework

Let's begin this journey with an introduction to The Follow Your Curiosity Framework. Then learn about each step in the following chapters to move toward new possibilities!

The Follow Your Curiosity Framework

Step 1. Uncover your curiosities.
Step 2. Explore by asking powerful questions.
Step 3. Take one small step.

PART I

FOLLOW YOUR CURIOSITY ... YOUR IDEAS DEPEND ON IT

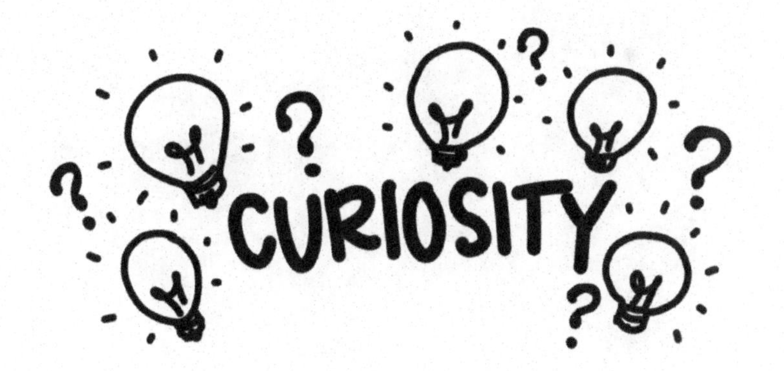

“Ideas come from curiosities.”

—Albert Einstein

CHAPTER ONE

Ideas Come to Us as Curiosities: Learn to Follow Them

Curiosity is an inherent part of human nature. From the moment we are born, we begin to explore the world around us, learning through our senses, experiences, and imagination. As young children, a curiosity tends to lead us to take an action that leads to another curiosity. We keep learning and exploring with each subsequent step forward. As we grow older, unfortunately, many of us lose touch with our innate curiosity. We learn to conform to societal expectations, become focused on achieving specific goals, follow routines, and the fear of judgment and failure sets in. We replace our natural wonder and intuition with mental and physical boundaries that we think keep us safe, but in doing so, we unintentionally lose the ability to follow our curiosity.

Think back to your childhood. How much more freely did you follow your curiosities in comparison to now as an adult? Growing up in the 1980s, I often played outside with my sister and brother independent of adult supervision, and we had plenty of opportunity to follow one curiosity to the next, leading to endless adventures and possibilities. There was the time we were curious about where the neighborhood stray cat came from. One day, we followed the scraggly orange tabby cat to a construction site nearby. That site became our daily playground and fort. We spent hours upon hours there, using our imagination to make up stories, play games, and simply explore. In hindsight, it gave us a place to create some of our most cherished early childhood memories. How about you? Think of a time you followed an impulsive curiosity as a child. What possibility did it open up for you? What memories did you make?

As kids, we innately rely on our curiosities to explore the world around us, often without hesitation. Now, as adults, our curiosities are initially followed by evaluation and second-guessing, versus intuitive action. But curiosity is not just for kids. As responsible adults, we may not have the luxury to be as impetuous and spontaneous in following our curiosities, yet we can still find ways to take action on the inquiries that tap us on the shoulder. They just might lead us to our very own metaphorical construction site that can become a playground for our imagination, creating space for novel personal and professional possibilities.

Being the mom to a young and wild boy has made me acutely aware of the stark contrast in curiosity between children versus adults. During hikes or even short walks around our neighborhood, my son often stops to explore, ask questions, or observe things beyond the beaten path. While he lives in a present state of wonder, my mind races ahead to the next item on our schedule or my endless to-do list. However, his relentless curiosity often prompts me to slow down to the here and now, and I also begin to take a closer look at the little things that catch my attention.

As a result, I start noticing common place things, like the crack in the sidewalk or the veins in a leaf, from new perspectives. It is in these moments that I realize that my curiosity is alive and well—often just overshadowed by the weight and responsibilities of adulthood—yet patiently waiting for me to pay attention.

I have yet to find or read a study that indicates that our human trait of curiosity naturally deteriorates over time. In fact, curiosity appears to be a stable personality trait that is present in people from a very young age, remaining relatively stable across our lifespan. Even if we are out of practice noticing and acting on our curiosities as adults, our curious nature is still there, waiting to be re-ignited and explored. That exploration, as you will come to see, has led me to possibilities that were brought to reality only through following my curiosities. The "Follow Your Curiosity" framework I am about to share with you will help you do the same.

Why Curiosity Matters

When we are curious, we are motivated to discover, investigate, and seek out new experiences and knowledge. Curiosity drives us to ask questions, to challenge assumptions, requiring us to think outside the box. You would be surprised at how many experiences, decisions, and life-shaping accomplishments can be attributed to curiosity.

Let's take time for reflection on how curiosity has impacted your life—and give it some credit!

Reflect on How Far Curiosity Has Already Taken You

Go to your workbook in the back of this book or download a copy at www.worksmartadvantage.com/whatifpigscanfly.

1. Grab a pen, or markers to get colorful!
2. In the left-hand column, jot down a few of your accomplishments.
3. In the right-hand column, identify the initial curiosity that led you there.

Examples from my life:

ACCOMPLISHMENT	CURIOSITY
☑ WRITING THIS BOOK	COULD I MAKE A BIGGER IMPACT WITH MY WORK?
☑ LEARNING TO PADDLE BOARD	HOW COULD I GET EXERCISE AND BE ON THE OCEAN?
☑ SPEAKING ON A TEDx STAGE	I WONDER IF I COULD SHARE MY STORY WITH MORE PEOPLE

Through this reflection, you may have noticed that curiosity plays a part in our lives even when we are unintentional about it. If that's the case, imagine how powerful curiosities can be when we intentionally pay attention to them and deliberately take small steps in their direction.

I once spoke at an insurance industry conference on the topic of following curiosities to explore ways of improving employee engagement and retention. The attendees were business owners and highly successful leaders in their parent organization. Following my talk, a gentleman approached me and light-heartedly remarked that no one dreams of becoming an insurance broker. I challenged him to reflect specifically on his own experience and the curiosity that initially led him to this field. It turns out that this was his second career—a shift prompted by a curiosity that whispered, "Could I explore a different career that would make a greater impact and allow me to spend more time with my family?" This curiosity widened his perspective, opened up his lens to the world of opportunities around him, and eventually led him down an unexpected path when over a family dinner, his sister-in-law was talking about how her career as an insurance agent gave her the flexibility to create meaningful impact for her family and her community. Because he had already primed his awareness around his curiosity, rather than saying "pass the butter" and letting this conversation be in passing, he followed up with more conversations with his sister-in-law and researched the field. Ultimately starting his own career as an insurance broker. He is now one of the most successful agents in the company—and is spending more time with his family and contributing to his community. A possibility made available to him through a curiosity.

I share this example to highlight the various forms curiosity can take. It can be grand, daring, and captivating; and it can also manifest as a simple, quiet question that leads to new unassuming possibilities. Regardless of its appearance, one thing holds true: Curiosity is a powerful catalyst for each of us to create remarkable and transformative experiences for ourselves and others.

Curiosity matters because when we are curious, we are more open-minded and receptive to new ideas and perspectives. We are more likely to ask questions, adapt to changing circumstances, and find creative solutions to problems.

There is also a sense of challenge and creativity in every curiosity, because curiosities encourage us to explore opportunities that are new and unknown to us, forcing us to think differently and get out of our comfort zones. Therefore, an added benefit of following our curiosities is that we also get to develop our creativity and courage. And couldn't we all use a little more of both?

Curiosity can be grand, daring, and captivating; and it can also manifest as a simple, quiet question that leads to new unassuming possibilities.

To add to my argument that curiosity matters, the next page reveals some benefits of living a curious life. Highlight the ones that are meaningful and beneficial to you, making sure to include your own ideas.

Bruce Lee said, "Absorb what is useful, discard what is useless, and add what is specifically your own."

As this book is about following your curiosity, I encourage you to retain the spirit of this quote as you work through the exercises. Take from it what is useful, what sparks your curiosity, make it your own—and leave behind the rest.

Benefits of Curiosity

- **Increased knowledge and understanding:** Curiosity drives us to seek out new information and perspectives, which can lead to a deeper understanding and appreciation of the people, experiences, and world around us.
- **Enhanced creativity:** Curiosity inspires us to think outside the box and come up with novel ideas and approaches to challenges and opportunities.
- **Improved problem-solving skills:** When we are curious, we are more likely to explore multiple solutions to a problem rather than settling for the first one that comes to mind.
- **Better relationships:** When you practice curiosity in communication, you are a better listener, which can improve empathy and relationships with others.
- **Increased adaptability:** Curiosity allows us to be more open to change and new experiences, which can help us adapt more easily to a variety of situations.
- **Greater happiness and fulfillment:** Curiosity can bring a sense of excitement and purpose to life as we pursue our natural interests.

Add your own:

____

____

Embrace Your Curiosity

Despite the benefits of curiosity, many of us struggle to maintain our curiosity as we take on the responsibilities of being an adult. Bogged down in the day-to-day demands of our lives, we may feel like we don't have the time or energy to explore new ideas or pursue our interests. The reality is, there are many ways to follow your curiosity—no matter your age, time constraints, or circumstances. Remember, your ideas depend on it!

Have you ever had a moment where you saw a commercial, passed by a storefront, or heard about a new product or service and thought to yourself, "Hey, that was my idea!"? You're not alone. Because we are all innately curious and creative, everyone has great ideas, but not everyone brings their ideas to life. The difference between those who do and those who don't starts with paying attention—paying attention to the ideas that come to us in the form of a curiosity.

Back when I was a freshman at UC Santa Barbara living in the dorms, parents would send their college kids boxes packed with everyday essentials like shampoo, conditioner, snacks, and Top Ramen (which was indeed a dorm staple!). These care packages sparked my curiosity: "What if I created a business where parents could select from a catalog of items, and I directly ship them to their kids?"

I never did pursue this idea because it seemed overwhelming for a 17-year-old college student to undertake. I let my overwhelm, doubt, and fear squash my curiosity. Looking back, if I had the "Follow Your Curiosity" framework, I could have called upon the tools to take at least one small step toward that curiosity. Who knows? Following that curiosity and taking a small step forward might have turned into a thriving company rivaling Amazon!

Many of us have had similar experiences, feeling as if we missed out on the potential of a curiosity. It's easy to dwell in regret, but the reality is that missing out on a curiosity is unavoidable since we have so many of them. I encourage you to let go of regrets about any so-called missed opportunities and focus on the curiosities that are currently tapping you on the shoulder. When it comes to curiosity, there will always be more. And if that curiosity you think you missed out on is still whispering to you, it's never too late to explore it.

Ideas Come to Us as Curiosities. Let's Identify Some of Yours

I propose that we are fascinated by certain curiosities because those specific curiosities are meant for us. We are intended to pay attention to them and follow their path to discover where they might lead us.

Each of us is unique and our curiosities reflect that. Picture a reality where we are free from the burden of conforming to predefined standards of success. Imagine if, instead of feeling like we need to reach for accomplishments that gain the accolades of social acceptance, we each pursue our innate curiosities and create unique outcomes distinctively meant for us. While I acknowledge that this is an idyllic scenario, I firmly believe that if each of us learns to follow our curiosities, we can create a more fulfilling life. Now, with this book in your hands, you have a set of tools and someone in your corner to begin turning this possibility into reality.

Your next curiosity just might be a great idea waiting to be explored and brought to life by a human partner–and that idea has chosen you.

To begin recognizing your curiosities, start by identifying your areas of interest. What topics or activities do you find yourself drawn to? What questions do you have about the world around you?

Take time now to answer the questions below and uncover your curiosities.

Brainstorm Your Curiosities

Reflect on interests and ideas that spark your curiosity. Use the prompts below to guide your brainstorming. Think of this as a creative art project. Pick a couple of the bullet pointed ideas below to bring creativity to this exercise:

- Rather than writing your ideas in a linear fashion, draw clouds on a piece of blank white paper and fill in those clouds with your curiosities. Or download the workbook at www.worksmartadvantage.com/whatifpigscanfly.
- Use markers rather than a pen or pencil.
- Sketch your answers.
- Grab magazines, a pair of scissors, and a glue stick. Collage your answers.
- Interview yourself—or ask people who know you well enough to answer these questions about you.

Prompts:

1. What topics or activities do you enjoy reading or learning about?
2. What questions do you find yourself asking about the world around you?
3. What are questions that keep coming back to you?
4. What experiences or moments in your life have sparked your curiosity?
5. What hobbies or interests have you always wanted to pursue but have not had the chance to?
6. If you had unlimited time and resources, what would you explore or learn more about?

The previous exercise was designed for you to identify some of your current and past curiosities. Keep this exercise handy as we will return to it further along in the book when we start to explore the steps to move forward with a curiosity.

In the next chapter, we tackle the practice of noticing your curiosities in the present moment. Because as stated earlier, our ideas come from curiosities, and from my experience, curiosities come to us in their own timing, for a reason. Your next curiosity just might be a great idea waiting to be explored and brought to life by a human partner—and that idea has chosen you. Let's explore ways to notice those ideas and curiosities in real time so they don't pass you by.

CHAPTER TWO

Wondering and Wandering: Leave Room for Curiosity

Warren Berger, author of *A More Beautiful Question*, states that children between the ages of 2 and 5 years old ask an average of 40,000 questions. If you've been around a child that age, you know that those wonderings usually start with "How?" or "Why?" These are the beginnings of verbalizing curiosities. You might also notice that children that age do a lot of wandering, letting every curiosity distract them and draw their attention. In other words, children are natural wonderers and wanderers.

As adults, we still possess that natural predisposition to wonder and wander, but we often spend our days preoccupied with our busy schedules. As a result, we can become disconnected from our intuitive thoughts and curiosities. Realistically, as grownups, we have significantly more responsibilities than children do. Consequently, as expected our opportunities to wonder and wander do not come as freely. Our days are filled with work, getting the kids ready for school, feeding the pets, going to the grocery store, answering emails, paying bills, and more. Yet, it is absolutely possible to be a responsible adult *and* continue to keep our minds open to curiosity.

As my 10-year-old son likes to say, "I might have to grow old, but I don't have to grow up!" This chapter highlights that mindset of sustaining a childlike sense of wonder and curiosity. It provides practical techniques for fostering this way of life despite our busy daily lives.

The process begins by allowing yourselves to slow down enough to reconnect to your natural state of wondering and wandering, much like you did when you were a 4-year-old.

Wondering and wandering allow for curiosity to tiptoe in.

Wonder

I wonder how many times curiosity has visited you—yet you were too busy to pay attention.

Our curiosities often arrive as questions that start with "How" or "Why," just as they did when we were kids. As kids, we were simply better at paying attention to them because not much else required our focused attention. As adults though, just as we may now need the help of a little extra light or our glasses to read the small print on a restaurant menu—with our concentration scattered among all our responsibilities—we may need a little help to pay attention to our curiosities. And that starts by recognizing what curiosity looks like and sounds like. Once you identify that, you can start appreciating that your curiosities are everywhere.

There is a phenomenon called Baader–Meinhof. It refers to biased attention toward an idea or a thing you've recently become aware of or have recently learned about. Once this new thing is on your brain's radar, you seemingly encounter it more frequently than before.

The phenomenon is also referred to as selective attention. Selective attention exists because our brain has limited capacity to process all the information we receive from our environment. Consequently, it focuses on noticing and retaining certain information while filtering out other data. You can imagine what a sensory overload it would be if your brain tried to process every bit of information it receives—from the bird singing in a tree 100 yards away to every word you hear while walking down a New York City sidewalk. Selective attention can help us to focus on bringing certain things to the forefront of our consciousness.

When we learn or become aware of something new, our brain creates a mental model or template for that information, which makes it easier for us to recognize and process it in the future. This heightened sensitivity can make it seem like the frequency of the thing we are noticing has increased, when in fact, it has remained the same all along, our brains are now just more adept to noticing it.

An example of selective attention might be when you are looking to buy a car then everywhere you go, you start seeing the make and model of the car you've been considering. More than likely, there has not been a sudden increase in the number of those cars on the streets; rather, your brain has selected to become more attuned to noticing that specific car.

You can also look at the Baader-Meinhof phenomenon as a way to actively model your thinking behavior. For instance, if you intentionally decide to practice positive thinking, let's say through meditation or a daily mantra, you might finally notice that the mural you drive by every day on your way to work isn't just an abstract painting but includes a quote about gratitude. In the context of curiosity, now that you are diving into this book and honing in on developing your curiosity, you might find yourself naturally recognizing your curiosities more often, giving your curiosity radar a boost.

Let's fine-tune your selective attention toward your curiosities by becoming familiar with how they show up. Here is a list of what your curiosity might sound like. Next time you notice a thought starting with one of the phrases below, pause and take note that this might be a curiosity asking to be explored.

- What if...?
- Why does...?

- How does...?
- What happens when...?
- Is it possible to...?
- What would happen if...?
- I wonder if...?

As we are all unique, our individual experience with curiosity also has its own fingerprint. In what other ways does curiosity tap you on the shoulder? Write those down and maybe even take the time to turn this exercise into the creative activity on the following page.

Grounding Rocks

In my team and leadership development workshops, we conclude sessions by making Creative Artifacts. These tangible items serve as a reminder of the key takeaways of the work we accomplished during the workshop. One example of a Creative Artifact we make is called Grounding Rocks.

To remind yourself of what your curiosities sound like, get some flat river rocks and paint markers at your local arts and crafts store. Decorate them with words and images that remind you to pay attention to your curiosities. If you're motivated to, buy a whole bag of rocks and design a rock every time you are inspired to do so throughout the course of reading this book. By the time you get to the last page, you could have your own rock garden filled with creative and curious inspiration.

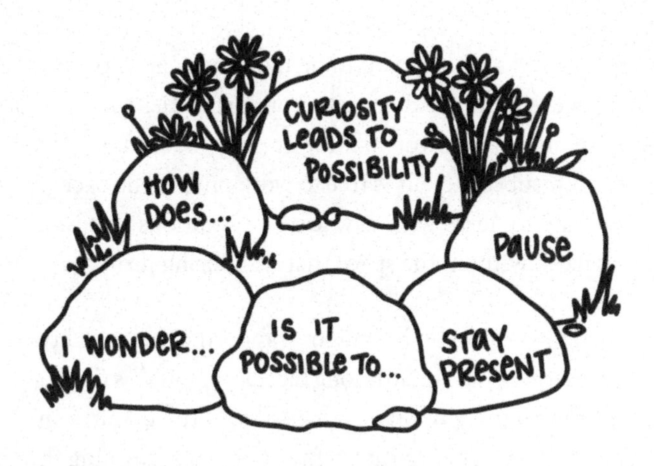

Wander

Gandalf from *The Fellowship of the Rings* said, "Not all who wander are lost."

I think in our busy lives, it is the act of wandering itself that has gotten lost. There are two types of wandering: physical wandering, where you hop on your bicycle and ride off without a destination or a plan, and mind wandering, where we mentally detach and stray from the task at hand.

Both types of wandering allow for curiosity to tiptoe in; because wandering in both forms allows your mind to break free from the constraints of your usual routine and thought patterns. When you wander, you are not focused on a specific goal or task, and your mind is free to explore and make connections between unconnected things, places, and ideas. Your unconscious ideas have room here to rise to the level of consciousness.

Wandering can also help you to be more present in the moment, creating space to notice details and opportunities that you might otherwise miss. When you are not intently focused on a problem or task, your subconscious is free to work on it in the background, and you may come up with new ideas or solutions that would not have surfaced without the space that wandering provides.

I have benefited from both types of wandering. In 2007, I traveled through Vietnam on a month-long bicycle ride. It was the first time I visited my country of birth since we fled the country in 1975, which you'll hear more about later in the book. Traveling through a country that I had last seen when I was 2 years old without much planning or knowledge of where I was going created a perfect environment for me to both physically and mentally wander. It was during those 30 days of peddling miles and miles a day, present in the moment, that I initially thought up the idea of bringing creativity to adult learning. Although it took me many more years to mold that initial idea into a reality, it was in that act of wandering where the curiosity first found me.

Overall, wandering can be an effective way to cultivate curiosity and generate fresh ideas by freeing your mind from routine and allowing it to explore and make new connections.

In a study conducted by Benjamin Baird and Jonathan Schooler, psychologists from the University of California, Santa Barbara, (my alma mater - Go Gauchos!) it was discovered that creativity is enhanced when the mind is allowed to wander in-between tasks, rather than simply taking breaks or engaging in other attention-demanding activities.

The researchers presented 145 undergraduate students with two "unusual uses" tasks. These tasks required participants to come up with as many unconventional applications as they could think of for everyday objects like toothpicks, clothes hangers, and bricks within a two-minute time frame. Once the initial task was completed, the participants were given a 12-minute break.

During the break, the students were divided into four different groups. One group rested, while another was asked to complete a challenging memory activity that required their full concentration. The third group engaged in an undemanding activity specifically designed to let their minds wander. The fourth group had no break at all.

At the end of the 12 minutes, all participants were asked to repeat the initial "unusual uses" task. The students who had participated in the undemanding "mind-wandering" activity performed an average of 41% better on the repeated task compared to their initial attempt. In contrast, students in the other three groups showed no statistically significant improvement.

The findings of this study point out the benefits of embracing moments of mind wandering as a channel to foster creativity. And creativity and curiosity come hand in hand. Curiosity initiates the creative process, while creativity nurtures and amplifies our curiosity. It's a positive feedback loop that has the ability to generate unique solutions and possibilities.

Here are some ideas to help you get started on your wandering journey. Pick one to do daily, weekly, or monthly to make wandering first a practice, and then a habit. As usual—add your own brilliant ideas!

- **Explore your neighborhood:** Take a walk or bike ride in your neighborhood noticing things that you haven't taken time to see, hear, or smell before. Become an observer of your environment.
- **Take the scenic road:** Choose a different path to work or places you usually go. Change up your routine.
- **Take a hike:** Nature has a positive impact on one's mood and can boost creativity. Go out into nature, see what curiosities come up.
- **Explore new places:** As creatures of habit, we tend to stick to what we know. Instead, head out to a new restaurant, neighborhood, city or country and see what you might find, or what finds you!

- **Get lost on purpose:** Sometimes the best way to wander is to not have a plan at all. Just pick a direction and start walking or driving, and see where the day takes you.

The Wall Street Journal published an article in 2022 titled The Emotional Benefits of Wandering, referencing a study led by Catherine Hartley of New York University that combined GPS data with happiness ratings to investigate the relationship between wandering and emotional well-being. The study involved over 100 participants from New York and Miami who agreed to share their phone's GPS data for three months while regularly rating their mood through an app.

The researchers used a measure called "roaming entropy" to analyze the GPS data, capturing the diversity and novelty of each participant's location. They then compared the roaming entropy data with the participants' self-reported mood ratings. The findings revealed that contributors who had higher roaming entropy, meaning they wandered and roamed to more novel and diverse places, reported increased well-being. The study also showed that the more you wander in a day predicts how happy you are later on, but not vice versa. In other words, being happy doesn't cause you to wander. But wandering does increase your happiness.

So go ahead and allow your mind and body to wander. It's good for you and your curiosity!

CHAPTER THREE

The Curiosity Journal: Wild and Crazy Ideas Welcomed!

Curiosities are those whispers that pop into our minds then vanish just as quickly as we move from one responsibility or distraction to another. The most effective way to capture these fleeting thoughts is to write them down. I keep a small physical journal to jot down my ideas and curiosities. You might choose to do the same, or maybe use a notetaking app on your phone or tablet. The format you use is a personal preference, as long as you get those curiosities out of your head and onto paper (or screen). I have found this to be the best way to capture curiosities exactly as they are in the moment. Whether those impulsive thoughts and ideas end up being meaningful or not, by writing them down, they have the chance to be remembered and materialized, rather than drifting off as a passing thought. The intent of writing your curiosities down as they come to you is not to capture them as concrete and complete ideas. Instead, it is to utilize them as prompts for further ideation, imagination, and creativity. The act of writing them down as is, without judgment, is a practice in Divergent Thinking.

There are two paired principles in the practice of creative problem solving called Divergent and Convergent Thinking. I will explain Divergent Thinking in more detail here and leave Convergent Thinking for later when it becomes applicable to the framework of following your curiosities.

Divergent Thinking

Divergent thinking is the process of generating as many ideas as possible without judgment. Evaluation through a set of constraints and parameters comes later in the convergent thinking process. Divergent thinking can be used individually or collectively to generate creative and unique solutions to overcome a challenge or vet an opportunity. It is creative and imaginative in nature. Some of the hallmark features of divergent thinking are:

- Free flow of ideas
- No judgment or criteria is placed on the ideas presented
- Wild and crazy ideas are welcomed
- Quantity of ideas are valued over quality

When we can notice, write down and capture our curiosities as an influx of divergent ideas—diverse and unrefined—we can then start to interconnect those ideas into possibilities. Since curiosities come to us as is—without fine-tuning or calculation, by using the principle of divergent thinking, we can approach them with an open mind instead of labeling and dismissing so-called crazy ideas and curiosities. Don't judge or reject them even if they don't make sense in the moment. These wild and impractical curiosities, if nurtured, could be the seeds that grow into your next big breakthrough.

Here's an example I often use when I teach divergent thinking to workplace teams. Imagine you're in a meeting with your CEO and colleagues, and your CEO poses a challenge to the group, asking for ideas to solve a current problem. When someone offers a solution, the typical response is to judge it on the spot with comments like, 'That's a good idea, but we don't have the time,' or the idea-killing phrase 'Yes, but…'.

This type of quick judgment along with an immediate critical comment shuts down ideas prematurely. When we present and judge ideas simultaneously, as in this example, we are in essence shooting down a curiosity before it has had the chance to reach its full potential. The divergent and convergent thinking framework proposes that we allow all ideas to be captured as is—in divergent thinking. All ideas make it to the table. Only when all ideas have been presented free of judgment do we move to the process of assessing and narrowing down ideas in convergent thinking.

Similar to the meeting room example above, we tend to use the same quick judgment and critique towards our own ideas too soon without giving them a chance to develop and be explored. Instead of the CEO or a colleague shutting us down, we are the ones evaluating our own curiosities as quickly as they arise, preventing us from seeing the potential even in our very own ideas and curiosities.

If you're kicking yourself for doing this, don't. It's human nature to immediately start mentally evaluating pros and cons. We all do it. Maya Angelou said, "Do the best you can until you know better. Then, when you know better, do better." So now that we know better, we can start to do better.

When the divergent thinking process is applied to the meeting room situation or our own curiosities, it allows all ideas to be heard without judgment. In divergent thinking, all ideas make it to the table without criticism or judgment. Whether written in a journal, on post-it notes, a whiteboard, or even constructed out of LEGO® bricks or play doh (which are tools I use with clients), all ideas are welcome and all ideas are captured as is.

Remember, most curiosities are not going to appear as succinct and viable ideas, but all curiosities are possible game-changers that deserve to be captured and given the time, attention, and opportunity to be developed.

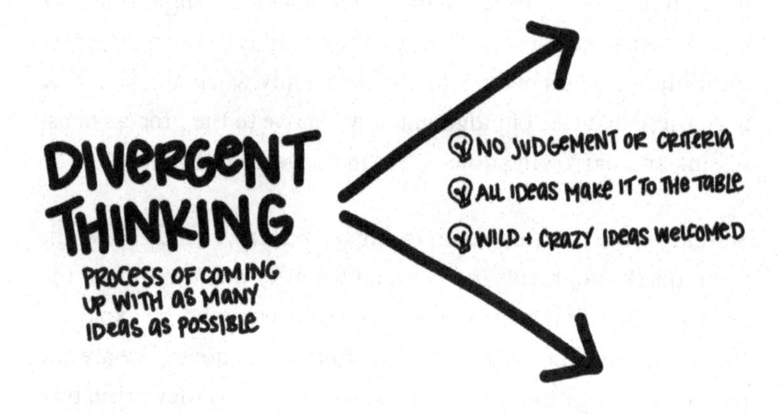

Get yourself that journal, or open up a new note on your phone and start jotting down your curiosities. Use the tool and mindset of divergent thinking as you begin a practice of writing down all the curiosities and ideas that come to you starting today, without filtering. All ideas make it to the table—or in this case, to your journal. Your objective here is simply to make your invisible thoughts, visible—to get your curiosities out of your head and make them tangible to be seen and revisited.

You might even want to schedule time, every now and then, to sit down with a cup of tea or coffee and skim through your journal. See if there is a throughline, a thread that connects your notes and ideas. Consider it a date with your curiosities.

Practice Divergent Thinking

Divergent thinking is the process of generating as many ideas as possible without evaluation. Practice divergent thinking with this exercise. Below you see an image of a clothing iron. Ask yourself, "What is this used for?" Your first response will most likely be, "Ironing clothes." Now ask yourself, "What else?" and let your imagination run wild. Remember the hallmarks of divergent thinking are that all ideas make it to the table, there is no judgment or criteria, and seek quantity over quality. Come up with as many uses for this iron as you can.

This exercise will give you the experience of thinking divergently. Practice the process of coming up with ideas—possibly wild and crazy—letting them take shape without judgment.

So far, you have learned to create moments of pause in your busy life to cultivate and observe your curiosities and become familiar with how they appear and what they sound like. Maybe you even took time to complete the creative exercise of making grounding rocks. You have also gained helpful tips to allow yourself to wander and wonder. And you were introduced to divergent thinking, a tool that requires you to be voraciously curious and creative without judgment.

Now it's time to start asking powerful questions. Mastering the art of asking thought-provoking and open-ended questions will lead you to identify your first small step toward fulfilling your curiosity and unlocking the possibilities it holds.

PART II

THE POWER OF "WHAT IF?"

"There is freedom waiting for you,
On the breezes of the sky,
And you ask, "What if I fall?"
Oh, but my darling, "What if you fly?"

—Erin Hanson

CHAPTER FOUR

Turn Curiosity into Creativity by Asking Powerful Questions

Your Brain Is a Search Engine

Ask it the right questions and your brain will lead you to endless possibilities. By framing questions that allow for open-ended responses, we give ourselves permission to think bigger and more creatively, directing our attention toward imagination and inspiration to find solutions and discover new opportunities.

Oftentimes, we don't ask big enough questions. Or when we do, and we come up with a big idea, our protective brain shuts it down right away. How many times have you come up with an idea that lights you up, and then within seconds, a voice in your head says something like, "That's not going to work" or "That's impossible!"

To turn curiosity into creative ideas, we need to learn to ask powerful questions and then give ourselves permission to practice divergent thinking. Let your imagination wander and embrace all kinds of wild thinking without judgment. That way, you can explore every possibility with an open mind and without restrictions. Even the craziest ideas that may not seem valid at face value may surprise you and turn into amazing and valuable insight. Give every idea a chance to take flight and see where it takes you!

I'm sure you have heard the saying, "There is no such thing as a stupid question." That may be true, *and* some questions are more powerful than others. Powerful questions have the ability to broaden our thinking, stimulate exploration and imagination, and help us in problem-solving and solution-finding.

In his book *A More Beautiful Question*, Warren Berger states that powerful questions can challenge our assumptions and help us to see beyond our current limitations. To quote him, "The most powerful questions are those that tap into our sense of wonder and curiosity, inspiring us to explore new frontiers and discover new truths."

Here are examples of powerful questions you can apply to your curiosities:

- What if?
- How might I (we)?
- What else?

One of the hallmark programs I offer at worksmart Advantage, my team and leadership consultancy, is called Leadership Canvas™. It is a 12-month program designed for current and aspiring leaders to gain and strengthen the soft—or more suitably termed—power skills needed to lead their teams. The highlights of the program include the longitudinal design (development over time), the incorporation of creative learning methods—I call it Creative Integration—and facilitation by subject-matter experts. The development of this program is a result of me asking, "What else?".

I had been running my business primarily delivering one-off workshops, and in doing so, I recognized that there was more I could do to help organizations develop individual contributors into leaders, keep employees engaged, and reduce turnover. Having identified this need, I started asking myself, 'What else?' and explored through divergent thinking, which resulted in the development of this program. It addresses the long-term needs of companies aiming to attract, engage, and retain top talent through skill building.

The art of asking powerful questions is a practice that I continue to work on as it does not necessarily come naturally to all or any of us. For example, I wholeheartedly believe in the benefits of Leadership Canvas™, yet doubts still crept in about whether or not companies would see the value in it to become a viable revenue stream to add to my offerings. One day, talking to my business coach, I asked, "Do you think this has potential to be profitable?" She responded with, "Ask a bigger question."

Putting thought on that request, I realized I was not using my brain as a search engine to find possibilities; rather, my question addressed my doubts and fears of potential failure. Acknowledging that, my new bigger question became, 'How might I use Leadership Canvas™ to make a greater impact?' This expansive question led me to imagine all the people and companies I could create positive change with through the program, allowing me to get creative and confident in how I talk about Leadership Canvas™ when reaching out to prospective clients.

Once I clarified the 'why' for Leadership Canvas™ by asking myself a more powerful question, it became easy to generate divergent ways my team of subject-matter experts and facilitators could add value to organizations through this particular program. Ideas flowed easily. With each new concept, I visualized how the program could positively impact others. Talking to people about it was not solely about business development or gaining clients—the conversations revolved around the specific needs of each organization and my mission of using creativity, longitudinal learning, and subject-matter experts as effective tools for adult learning. Conversations became a co-creation of ideas about how my services could help solve their challenges.

Leadership Canvas™ was not the first time asking powerful questions impacted my life. That happened years ago. Only in sharing the following family story in my TEDx Talk in 2019 did it dawn on me that following my curiosities, asking powerful questions, and taking small steps have become natural to me because at a very young age, I witnessed this framework create unforeseeable possibilities that changed my family's life, generate opportunities for thousands of other families, and spearhead the transformation of an entire industry.

Your brain is a search engine. Ask it the right questions and it will lead you to endless possibilities.

CHAPTER FIVE

Red Nail Polish

The manicure industry in the United States is an 8.3-billion-dollar industry, dominated by Vietnamese Americans who make up 51% of the profession across the nation and 80% in California.

And it all started with a curiosity about, of all things, red fingernail polish.

April 29,1975 marks the evacuation of United States military forces from Vietnam and the subsequent end of the Vietnam War one day later. My dad was a Lieutenant Colonel in the South Vietnamese Air Force, working alongside his US counterparts. On this day, with news of imminent defeat and the overrunning of Saigon by the North Vietnamese army, my father was dismissed from duty. He was told to go home and get his family out of the country any way he could. He rushed home to my mom and told her, "It's time. We have to get out, now." My parents grabbed their three children, all of us under the age of 4, packed one suitcase, and along with my aunt who was spending the night at our house, and my grandfather who lived with us, we fled, leaving behind friends, family, careers, possessions, and country.

As tanks rolled into Saigon and bombs flew overhead, we were among the fortunate ones who found a way out on one of the last two cargo planes leaving Tan Son Nhut Airbase. We landed on a small island where the US Navy was able to transport us to safety, and we became part of the first wave of Vietnamese refugees to enter the United States.

Our first home in America was Camp Pendleton Marine Base in San Diego. It was a whirlwind as service men and women on base had less than 36 hours to prepare for the arrival of a staggering 18,000 Vietnamese refugees. The Marines took care of us during our month-long stay at Camp Pendleton before we were transferred to our second home, Hope Village. Hope Village was a refugee integration center located in Weimar California, near Sacramento, run by a civilian organization called Food for the Hungry. The purpose of this center was to assist us in integrating into our new lives by providing job training, English lessons, and connecting us with sponsors from across the country. Hope Village became a stepping stone for my parents as they embarked on the journey to rebuild our lives in the United States. It was a place where out of necessity everyone was asking powerful questions to create new possibilities.

It was here at Hope Village that 20 Vietnamese refugee women met a Hollywood movie star, leading to a curiosity and a relationship that would make manicures an unexpected part of the Vietnamese American story.

Among those 20 women was my mom, Thuan Le. The Hollywood movie star was Tippi Hedren, most famously known for her starring role in Alfred Hitchcock's movie *The Birds*. Tippi volunteered at Hope Village, and as she puts it, "...just fell in love with these women," whose lives had been traumatically and permanently changed. She was determined to empower them to develop an employable skill, giving them a way to support their families. With this goal in mind, Tippi started a program that made typing and sewing classes available because these were skills that could be learned fairly quickly and there was a low barrier of entry into the workplace.

While participating in this program, where Tippi played an active role—the women noticed something that caught their attention and curiosity—Tippi's long red manicured fingernails. Given the circumstances, it would have been easy for Tippi and these women to ignore this curiosity and continue to focus on typing and sewing. Instead, their curiosity grew, leading Tippi to wonder, "What if we could get these women trained and licensed as manicurists?" Tippi shared this powerful question with my mom and the other women, and they started to ask "How might we?"

Their questions allowed their imagination to wander, and it also came with obstacles. For example, what beauty school would enroll 20 Vietnamese refugees who couldn't pay tuition? And most of these women didn't speak English. How would they read, understand, and pass their written test that was only available in English? And how could this all be done in the limited time they had at Hope Village?

Clearly, there were challenges. But they didn't focus on the impossibilities rooted in these challenges. Instead, they remained curious about the possibilities that lived in the questions "What if?" and "How might we?" Despite the hurdles, Tippi chose to take one small step forward and asked her personal manicurist, Dusty Coots Butera, if she would teach these women how to do a basic manicure. Dusty said yes, and on weekends traveled from Los Angeles to Hope Village to teach this group of women fundamental manicure techniques. My mom and her friends soaked up everything they were taught. They loved it, and they were good at it! Learning from Dusty did not make them licensed manicurists, but it was the first small step in the direction of their curiosity which opened up a door to the next step.

Continuing to follow curiosity, Tippi approached the owners of a nearby beauty school and inquired if there was any chance they would accept my mom and her friends as students, even though they faced language barriers and financial constraints. Becky and Charles Hamilton, the founders of Citrus Heights Beauty College found a way, and they also said yes.

Following curiosity by asking "What if?" and "How might we?", having the courage to take one small step forward, and the kindness of strangers allowed for this group of refugee women to complete 400 hours of schooling in 10 weeks and resulted in all of them passing their manicure practicum and written test in English—to become the first 20 licensed Vietnamese manicurists in the United States.

Soon after, a church generously sponsored our family's next step. They relocated us to Santa Monica, offered us assistance with housing and provided us with a community to lean on as my parents searched for employment and acclimated to our new reality. With fondness and gratitude, we said goodbye to Hope Village and moved to Southern California as my parents embarked on the journey of rebuilding our lives.

My dad found a job with the United Stated Post Office, and with her brand-new license in one hand and a letter of recommendation from Tippi Hedren in the other, my mom landed her first job as a manicurist at Beau Jacques Beauty Salon in West Los Angeles. At first, she struggled to grow her clientele. But with consistency, perseverance and curiosity, I watched her become a confident and capable entrepreneur who significantly contributed to our family's income. My parents moved us out of our two-bedroom, one-bath apartment into a four-bedroom condo, and within six years, they were home owners. The other women who had trained with my mom at Citrus Heights Beauty College followed similar paths around the country.

Tippi had set out to train these 20 women in a profession that would allow them to provide for their families. Her mission was accomplished. What Tippi and this group of women could not foresee was the impact their curiosity, powerful questions, and small steps would have on thousands of others.

Following the initial wave of refugees in 1975, a multitude of South Vietnamese persisted to seek refuge through immigration to the United States. The refugees and immigrants who arrived in those later years learned about the manicure profession from my mom and her friends, and their friends from them. This cycle of passing on the knowledge that this trade created a path to independence and stability continued as more Vietnamese women—and men settled across the country and became licensed manicurists. And over the past four decades, many of these Vietnamese Americans developed their own curiosities, prompting them to ask, "What if?"

What if we opened up our own salon?
What if we started our own beauty school?
What if we manufactured the supplies and tools we need?

Of those was my mom's high school friend Kien Nguyen who re-settled in the United States through a refugee center in Arkansas. When her family was sponsored to California, she came to visit my mom at work and from there embarked on her own "What if" path. Kien and her husband Minh Tam ultimately opened their own beauty school in Orange County in 1987. Now owned and operated by their son and daughter Tam and Linh, Advance Beauty College, in the past 36 years, has grown to include three brick-and-mortar locations and an online campus. They have trained over 50,000 manicurists—largely contributing to the Vietnamese manicure legacy across America.

They had lost everything, including their homeland, yet they still had the power of their curiosity.

The sum of thousands of "What if's," small steps, and determination amounts to the Vietnamese community's significant contribution to the growth and establishment of the manicure industry in the United States as it stands today—a thriving $8.3-billion-dollar industry.

This is a story of possibility, the possibility that is created when we follow our curiosity, ask expansive questions like "What if?" and "How might I?", and move forward with the courage to take the first small step in spite of the obstacles that stand in our way.

There's a saying, "Curiosity is the most powerful thing you own." For the original 20 women who became the first licensed Vietnamese manicurists in the United States, this proved to be true. They had lost everything, including their homeland, yet they still had the power of their curiosity. A power that created the possibility for them to craft a life for themselves in their new country.

This story of my mom and her friends has always inspired me. If this is what can be accomplished by inadvertently following a curiosity, I wonder what possibilities you might create for yourself and for others by deliberatively following your curiosity, asking significant questions such as "What if?" and taking one small step forward. Let's find out!

Take time now to explore your curiosities with the questions of "What if?" and "How might I?" as they are jam-packed with potential. The purpose of this exercise is to give you the experience of asking questions that encourage you to reach for possibilities. By asking "What if?" or "How might I?", you are making room for your curiosity and innate creativity to become fresh opportunities. Of course, remember to use the principle of divergent thinking. Your wild, ridiculous, and seemingly impossible ideas are encouraged!

Practice Powerful Questions: "What if?" and "How Might I?"

Start by writing one of the curiosities you brainstormed previously, or a new one that has whispered to you, in the center of a blank sheet of paper and circle it. Or use the worksheet provided.

Your curiosity could take the form of questions or statements such as:

- I wonder...
- I've always wanted to...
- There's this idea I have...

Next, jot down possibilities that could come from following that curiosity. To generate ideas, use your powerful questions of "What if?" and "How might I?" Write down your ideas starting with phrases like:

- I might …
- I could …
- It would be fun to …

To add creativity to the process, try sketching your ideas before putting words to them. This can help activate your imagination to generate more ideas.

Keep your process open and free from self-criticism to encourage creativity and innovation. Allowing yourself to think freely without judging or filtering your ideas can lead to unexpected and exciting discoveries. Don't be afraid to explore different possibilities and let your imagination run wild.

See my example below:

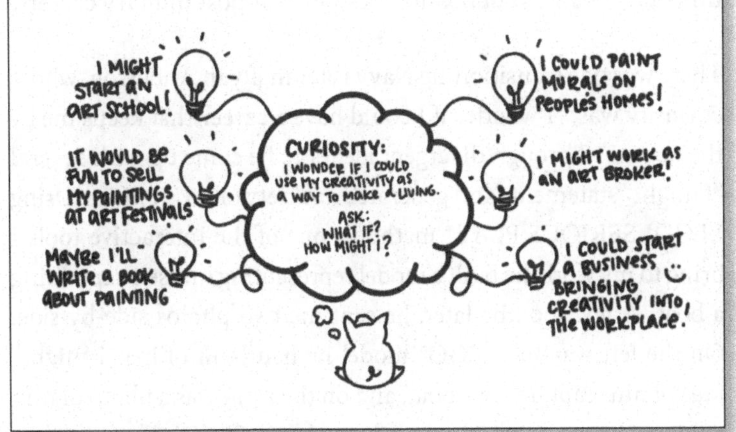

In my family's story, I shared that our first home in the United States was at Camp Pendleton Marine Base in San Diego. It's a full-circle experience for me to now bring my work to a non-profit organization called The Honor Foundation (THF). THF offers a three-month program preparing elite members of the United States Special Operations Forces including Navy SEALs, Marine Raiders, and Green Berets through their move from military to civilian careers. I teach a course called Transition Night, the last class before participants graduate from the program. The exercise you were just exposed to is similar to one I use in the THF class, where I invite these men and women to ask bigger questions and think creatively about possibilities for their post military careers.

There was one transitioning Navy veteran, Ryan Anderson, whose curiosity was, "I wonder if I could have a career that keeps me by the ocean?" Through divergent ideation, he came up with several "I might" statements and generated a variety of possibilities. Using LEGO® SERIOUS PLAY® methods, one of the interactive tools I bring to my work, he built a model representing himself captaining a boat. A few months later, he sent me two photos side-by-side. On the left was the LEGO® model he had built of his "I might" idea of him captaining a boat, and on the right was a photo of him enjoying his new career as a yacht broker in San Diego. This is the power of curiosity and asking bigger questions—your dreams and underlying aspirations can become your reality.

Curiosity will always require us to act with courage as it asks us to pursue something new and oftentimes outside our comfort zone.

It is not lost on me that all these years after the US Military played a major role in my family's transition from post-war Vietnamese refugees to thriving citizens of the United States, I now get to play a role in assisting service men and women with their transition from military to civilian careers. The way I secured this opportunity to become a volunteer faculty member at The Honor Foundation is, you guessed it, by following a curiosity. As a certified LEGO® SERIOUS PLAY® (LSP) methods facilitator and licensed trainer through an organization called Strategic Play, I am a member of their online network of facilitators. While scrolling the opportunities section of the community board, I came across a request for a LEGO® SERIOUS PLAY® facilitator in the San Diego area who could develop a program for veterans. As a new LSP facilitator at the time, I was both curious and intimidated by the opportunity. Despite the hesitation caused by my lack of experience, I leaned into the curiosity and reached out for more information. Within one brainstorming session over Zoom with Joe Lara, then the VP of Programming at The Honor Foundation, we agreed it would be a fit to bring LEGO® SERIOUS PLAY® methods to their program, specifically to get participants to think creatively as they consider possibilities for their future in a class titled Transition Night.

What I learned from taking action despite being intimidated by self-doubt and lack of experience is that curiosity will always require us to act with courage. It asks us to pursue innovation and change, oftentimes outside our comfort zone. Curiosity alone cannot create new possibilities; it must be followed by the courage of action. By taking even one small step, you are moving closer to making your ideas a reality. As seen in my experience with The Honor Foundation, following your curiosity might lead you to unexpected opportunities and life-fulfilling encounters. So, let's get back to our work together.

Having completed the last exercise, you now have applied powerful questions to one curiosity and have come up with a variety of practical and maybe impractical ideas to move forward. I hope you are feeling excited about the possibilities you've written down.

Now you are ready to identify and take your first small step.

PART III

THE MAGIC OF SMALL STEPS

"Take the first step in faith. You don't have to see the whole staircase, just take the first step."

—Martin Luther King, Jr.

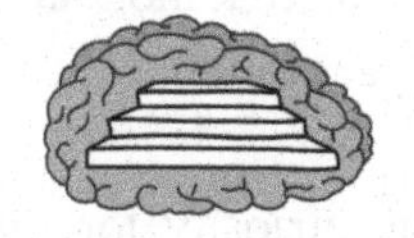

CHAPTER SIX

The Neuroscience of Small Steps

I was introduced to the neuroscience of taking small steps when I read Dr Robert Maurer's book, *One Small Step Can Change Your Life: The Kaizen Way.* In this small but mighty book, Maurer highlights the Kaizen philosophy, which stresses the significance of making incremental progress toward achieving our big objectives. By adopting this small step approach, we can overcome the brain's natural resistance to change, which often makes it challenging to accomplish goals.

Dr Maurer suggests that by taking small steps, we can develop momentum as we build positive habits that lead to long-term success. From a neuroscience perspective, this small step approach can be effective because it activates the brain's reward system, which releases the neurotransmitter dopamine.

Dopamine is associated with pleasure and reward; it is released in response to positive experiences, such as accomplishing a goal or taking even a small step toward a larger objective. By breaking down our goals into small, achievable steps, we trigger the regular release of dopamine and experience feelings of reward. This creates a positive feedback loop that motivates us to continue making progress toward our larger goals.

To illustrate, when the curiosity for my business, worksmart Advantage, first came to me, I felt both excited and overwhelmed. The novel idea of integrating creativity into the corporate world to foster team and leadership development was thrilling, different, and energizing. However, the prospect of starting a business from scratch, based on a concept that I made up out of curiosity, was daunting. I had no idea where to start or even how to obtain a business license, let alone run a successful company.

As my idea was a relatively leading-edge business concept, there was no established blueprint for me to follow, and I was flooded with self-defeating questions and concerns. I felt it was too big a mountain to climb, and it took me six years from inception to actualizing my business. I eventually started making progress when I began by taking one small step at a time toward my goal.

My first small step was an internet search on creativity at work. That search led me to finding Kaizen-Muse Creativity Coaching, an online certification course for creativity coaches developed by Jill Badonsky. I figured as a new mom with a full-time job, coaching individuals on their creative projects as a side gig would fit into my life. As I progressed through the course, I began using the tools I learned from the program to coach myself to move step by step toward creating my business. Using this small step approach, I developed a course called "Turn Your Values into Action" and piloted it as a workshop in my backyard with friends and family. Then I created another and hosted it at a friend's art studio and opened it up to the public. With the modest success and dopamine hit of each small step encouraging me on, I kept creating and taking incremental action. One day, as I was packing workshop supplies into the trunk of my car, my neighbor approached me, curious about my work. After that driveway conversation, she hired me for my first corporate workshop–at Google.

Looking back on this experience, I clearly see how every small step led to the next step and then bigger strides as I pivoted and iterated my business. With the accomplishment of each step, I gained more confidence in my ability and the value I was providing through my programs. On a neuroscience level, each small step I accomplished resulted in a release of dopamine, rewarding my actions and giving me the motivation to take the next step. It was the combination of persistence, determination, and a willingness to take action, no matter how small, and despite fear and challenges, that helped me launch my business—and keep going.

You just have to take that first step, even—and maybe especially—when the next step isn't yet clear to you.

A Small Step Success Story

Jacquie Lloyd Smith is the founder of Strategic Play – the organization with which I am certified as a LEGO® SERIOUS PLAY® methods facilitator and licensed trainer. We first crossed paths in 2017 at the Creative Problem Solving Institute (CPSI) conference in Buffalo, New York, where Jacquie led a series of engaging LSP workshops.

Fast forward to 2022, we were both back at CPSI. This time, not only did I attend, but I also had the privilege of being one of the workshop facilitators. Jacquie joined my "Power of Curiosity" session, during which I presented the "Follow Your Curiosity" framework. At the time, she was piloting her new Playsonality© Playstyles Program and was intrigued by the prospect of creating a product around it, given that it required trainers to have a specific set of supplies. She posed the question, "What if I got branded boxes?" and identified her first small step. In October 2023, I completed the Strategic Play training to become a certified Playsonality© facilitator. There, at the front of the room were branded boxes of Playsonality© materials, ready for each trainer to take home. Jacquie attributes the realization of this physical product to my workshop, this framework, and the decision to take that crucial small step forward.

I can give you another personal example—writing this book. Instead of setting an ambitious goal of writing for hours on end, I would tell myself to write for just 15 minutes a day. When these 15-minute blocks effortlessly flowed into 20 or 30 minutes, I felt a sense of accomplishment. It boosted my confidence, triggered the dopamine effect, and made it easy to keep writing.

In contrast, if I had set a goal of writing for three hours and ended up writing for two hours, I would feel like I had fallen short and would have been discouraged. Exceeding small goals helped me maintain the confidence and consistency to keep making progress. And it will work for you too, because it's science!

I mentioned earlier that when I initially conceptualized my business, I felt anxiety and overwhelm that prevented me from taking action. As Dr Maurer explains, the anxiety that leads to inaction is also based in neuroscience, particularly in an area of the brain called the amygdala. The amygdala is responsible for detecting and responding to potential threats or danger by activating the 'fight or flight' response.

When we contemplate making significant moves, our amygdala is triggered to protect us. I like to refer to the amygdala as our bodyguard. When we try activities outside our comfort zone, we awaken our bodyguard, who then sends signals that we are in danger through increased heart rate, breath rate, and those feelings of overwhelm and anxiousness. By taking the small step approach toward our big goals, we tiptoe around the amygdala, allowing ourselves to move forward in flow and progress faster toward our goals than attempting giant leaps, which often make us feel like we are going to fall through the gaps. As you progress on this journey of following your curiosity, pay attention to how you are feeling.

If you sense anxiety, worry, or find yourself frozen in inaction, it might be a sign that you are attempting a step too big for your nervous system. Possibly, a smaller step is needed.

Another aspect of the small step approach is that you just have to take that first step, even—and maybe especially—when the next step isn't yet clear to you.

I understand that the ambiguity of not knowing what's next is tough for many people. Think of the process of taking one small step at a time as a muscle that needs to be strengthened. There's a term in creative problem solving called "Creative Chaos," which refers to the time between the excitement of starting something new and the achievement of it. That in-between gap can cause unease due to the unknown.

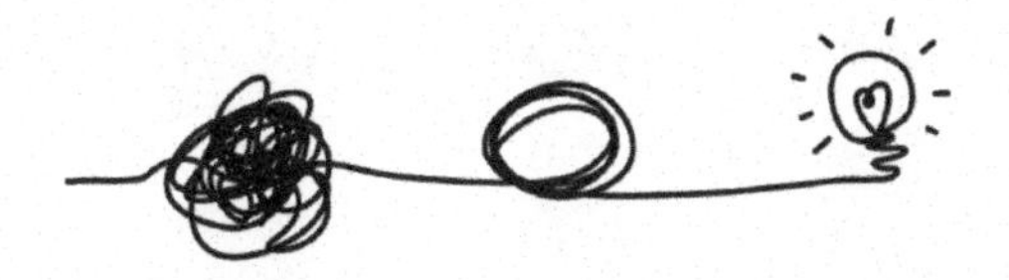

Creative chaos is entirely normal and will occur 100% of the time when you're starting something new, as well as when taking one step forward before you are clear on the subsequent steps. When it shows up, and it will, just remember that on the other side of that chaos is where the magic happens—innovation, change, new ways of thinking, and, of course, exciting possibilities. It can be argued that adopting a step-by-step approach to the process, rather than attempting to see the entire path, can actually aid in maintaining a sense of control and direction. Since all you need to focus on is the accomplishment of what is right in front of you.

CHAPTER SEVEN

The Domino Effect or The Universe Has Your Back

The act of setting up dominoes in a way that, when the first one is toppled, it triggers a chain reaction causing all the others to fall, is often referred to as "domino toppling" or "domino effect." Whether only a few dominoes or an extremely long and complicated path of hundreds of dominoes, the effect is the same. Once the first one is put into motion, it falls against the next, putting that one into motion and then the next, until the entire series is complete. One small action produces movement and the potential of massive shifts. I'm asking you to take a similar approach to your curiosities. Taking your first small step is knocking over that first domino to set off your own chain reaction.

Once you've taken that first small step, pay attention to the doors that open for you and look for the next step that appears. When it comes to following your curiosities, the act of taking your first small step can certainly lead to that domino effect. I purposely used the word "can" because it doesn't always mean it will. You might realize after taking one small step that this is not a curiosity you want to continue to follow, or that your original curiosity pivots entirely from what you originally imagined. On the other hand, after taking that first step you might find the next step naturally opening up for you, leaving you even more energized and excited to move forward. Regardless of how your curiosity takes shape, the beauty of curiosity is that there will always be more, and it always has the potential to take you somewhere you have not yet been. To borrow from a marketing sign I read on a people mover at Boston's Logan airport meant to encourage people to travel more—following curiosity shows you how to "cross paths with a road you haven't been down."

When you move in the direction of your curiosities and your dreams, the universe has your back.

Earlier, I shared that I landed my first corporate workshop because I took the small step of facilitating a program at my friend Gus Harper's art studio. My neighbor, who worked at Google, happened to see me packing supplies into the car, leading her to hire me for a team offsite. There was also the time I decided to step out of my comfort zone and attended a women's networking event in Santa Monica alone. I found myself sitting next to a woman named Mary Stuart. Our curiosities and conversation led us to uncover the fact that Jacob, her then-boyfriend (now husband), did work that complemented my creative style of leadership and team development by bringing play into the workplace. Since then, I have developed a great friendship with Mary Stuart and Jacob. Additionally, Jacob and I have collaborated to deliver team and leadership development programs across the country, both in-person and virtually, through worksmart Advantage and his company, I Make Work Fun!

Going back to my work as a volunteer faculty member at The Honor Foundation (THF), taking the small step of responding to a request on a LEGO® SERIOUS PLAY® facilitator forum—even when I did not feel qualified, led to the incredible opportunity to bring my creative work to THF's world-class military transition program. I have since had the honor of serving hundreds of members of the U.S. Special Operations Forces in their pursuit of a post military career. The relationships I have built through this program have led me to some of the most valued friendships and business partnerships I now enjoy.

It is because of experiences like these that I firmly believe when you move in the direction of your curiosities and your dreams, the universe has your back.

Another example of the universe having my back and the power of curiosity is evidenced in my experience getting onto a TEDx stage. That achievement began as a curiosity whispering to me when I was sitting in the audience of a Vietnamese manicure industry conference in Anaheim, California honoring Tippi Hedren and the women, including my mom, who created the opportunity for the industry's growth among the last three generations of Vietnamese Americans. I had always been curious about delivering a TEDx Talk. While sitting in the audience, I thought, "What if I could tell my mom's story on a TEDx stage?" With that, my intention was set, and I had a new curiosity to follow.

A few weeks later, I came across a LinkedIn post announcing a nearby TEDx Talk, TEDx Women: Mission of Mavericks, serendipitously being held in Anaheim—the same city where I had watched my mom being honored by the Vietnamese manicure community. The speakers were already selected for this TEDx talk. The organizers were simply selling audience tickets. I bought one then stepped away from my computer. And there it was, that tap on my shoulder whispering, "What if you could present on that TEDx stage?"

Equipped to recognize that question as a curiosity, rather than dismissing the idea, I decided to take one small step forward and emailed the organizer: 'I have a story I would like to share on your TEDx stage.' I went on to write a brief summary of my proposed talk. A couple of days later, I received a response: 'We would be honored to have you tell your story at our TEDx event.' By slowing down to recognize the connection between my curiosity and this opportunity, listening to the 'what ifs,' and having the courage to take a small step, I was able to create this possibility for myself.

That TEDx Talk has led to invitations to speak on dozens of stages, appear on podcasts, and even the opportunity to bring my mom to speaking engagements where she can hear me tell her story, see the influence it has had on me, and witness the reaction from people hearing it for the first time. That is priceless. The domino effect works, and the universe has your back, but only if you are willing to take that first small step, which will likely be outside of your comfort zone.

Each of the small steps I mentioned insisted that I move out of my comfort zone, and yours will too. Be brave, courageous, take action, starting with one small, out-of-your-comfort-zone, courageous step.

As we explore the first small step toward the curiosity you identified, let me introduce you to the second half of the divergent and convergent thinking principle.

Convergent Thinking

We previously defined and worked with the divergent thinking principle: generating fresh ideas by exploring many possible paths. Let's now look at convergent thinking, which is the opposite of divergent thinking.

Convergent thinking involves narrowing down possibilities, ideas, or solutions to find the best or most effective one to move forward with first. This thinking model is focused on selecting a single answer or resolution to a challenge or opportunity. For our purposes of following your curiosities, it means picking one small step to move forward with. We'll get into that in more detail later. In general, it's in the convergent thinking phase where you evaluate your options based on a set of parameters and criteria and make the choice to move forward. The characteristics of the convergent thinking process include:

- A narrowing down of ideas
- Setting parameters and criteria to filter your ideas
- Choosing one idea to move forward with

Very importantly, convergent thinking should only come into play once you have thoroughly explored all ideas using divergent thinking. I'm going to repeat that. Convergent thinking should only be put into practice after you have completed your divergent thinking process. Divergent and convergent thinking cannot effectively be executed simultaneously. Think about driving a car. You press the gas pedal when you want to go. You press the brake pedal when you want to stop. You won't get very far if you try to press both at once. The same principle applies to divergent and convergent thinking. You won't get very far if you execute both simultaneously.

Here's an example of how to effectively converge after you've diverged. Imagine you are back in that meeting with your CEO and colleagues brainstorming a solution to a challenge. After using divergent thinking to generate a range of ideas, the focus then shifts to convergent thinking. Together, you establish specific criteria that the solution must meet, such as budget constraints, time limitations, or alignment with company values. With these parameters in place, you evaluate all the ideas presented and decide on the one idea or combination of ideas that best meets the established criteria. Similarly, when applying convergent thinking to your personal curiosities, you are the CEO, and you get to establish the criteria and parameters to filter your ideas through.

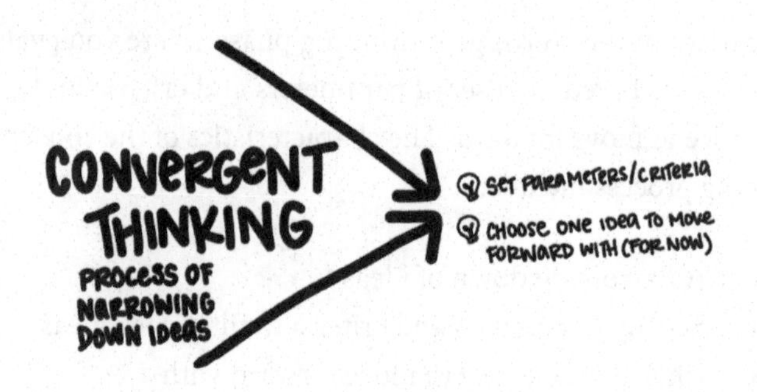

It's worth noting that just because the other ideas are not selected for implementation doesn't mean they're unworthy or invalid—they simply may not fit the specific parameters established for the particular situation at this moment in time. Yet they may come in handy in the future.

Let's test this out on your "I might" or "I could" statements you wrote down from the last exercise in Chapter 5 where you used divergent thinking to come up with as many possibilities as you could imagine around a single curiosity. We're going to filter those ideas through the convergent thinking process.

Pick a place to start!

Look at your "I might," "I could," and "It would be fun if" statements from the last exercise.

Follow these steps to filter your ideas through a set of criteria—in order to narrow down and identify the idea you want to move forward with—from there, you will create your first small step.

Step 1. Set your parameters. Write down three to four statements to filter your ideas through.

Step 2. Filter each of your "I might" statements through those parameters and see which make it across.

Step 3. If you still have more than one, pick the one idea that excites you the most to move forward with.

When making this decision, try using a technique I learned from a coach I worked with early on in my business. As I was trying to decide whether or not to move forward with an opportunity, he told me to ask my body, in addition to my mind. He encouraged me to feel the decision in my body and ask myself, "Is this a whole body hell, yes!". If the answer was indeed "yes," then move forward. If not, then it was a "hell, no" to the decision at hand.

For example, one of my "I might" statements when deciding on my business was "I might buy an old school bus and turn it into a mobile art studio for kids' birthday parties." My convergent parameters were:

1. Has to build on my current interests and skills.
2. Must bring me joy.
3. No working on weekends.

Therefore, the school bus idea did not make it because it didn't pass criteria number three, no working on weekends, and when I thought about if it would bring me joy, it was not a "hell, yes" in my body or my mind.

On the other hand, starting a business bringing creativity into corporate learning and development builds on my interests, absolutely brings me joy, and does not require me to work on weekends. This idea met all the criteria I set.

It's your turn to put this into practice. Use the 'One Small Step' section in your workbook to converge all your possibilities down to one idea to move forward on.

Using your own set of parameters, you have now narrowed down your divergent thinking options to a singular idea to move forward with. In my example above, the idea I narrowed down to was "start a business bringing creativity into corporate learning." Looking at that statement, I can recall feeling both excitement for the idea and overwhelm about actualizing it. It's here, in the gap between the excitement about the idea and the actualization that the purpose and magic of "one small step" takes shape.

Now that you have narrowed down to the one idea you want to move forward with, let's find one small step to get you started.

To find that small step, go through the divergent and convergent exercises again. Your workbook walks you through this step-by-step:

1. Use divergent thinking to brainstorm ideas regarding one small step you can take toward achieving your converged idea. Come up with as many small steps as you can to give yourself options. Recall that the characteristics of divergent thinking include: all ideas make it to the table, no judgment of ideas, and welcome wild and crazy ideas!
2. Once you are done ideating, move to convergent thinking. Set your criteria for filtering your small step ideas through. Then select the one small step you are going to start with.
3. Finally, commit to taking action on your small step and give yourself a timeline. Hint: If you are not able to commit to taking action on your small step within 48 hours, the step may not yet be small enough.

Using my example above of "starting a business bringing creativity into corporate learning and development," here's what the process looks like:

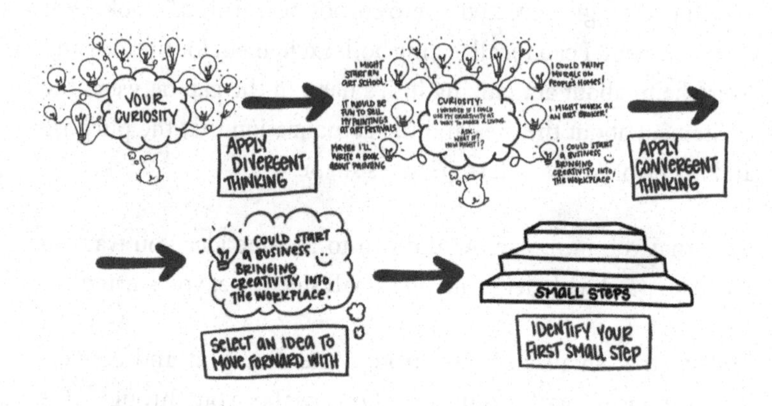

By simply jotting down that small step, you have in fact taken your first small step toward your curiosity. Congratulations! In my workshops, I not only request participants write down their small step; I also ask them to share that small step aloud to another person in the room. This approach is rooted in the belief that when we put an idea to paper, it begins to take shape. And when we speak it aloud, we generate more energy and enthusiasm, strengthening our commitment and propelling ourselves toward action. Remember, curiosities have to be followed by action to create possibilities. I encourage you to share your one step with someone who will be supportive, encouraging, and a cheerleader for your possibilities.

Now that you have identified your first small step, use the worksheet on the next page (or workbook) to begin your curiosity journey, starting with writing down your action item on the bottom step. Write out subsequent steps as they come to you, reaching your goal by climbing one small step at a time.

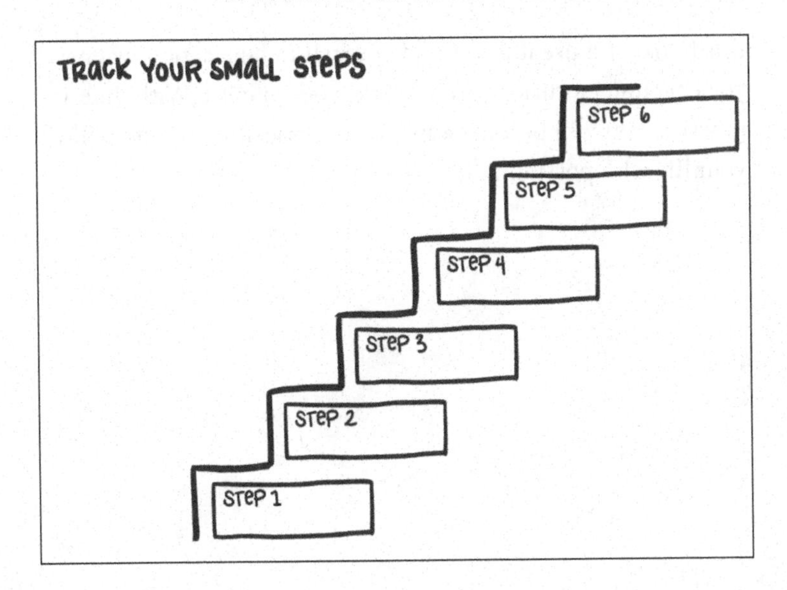

You have now learned the Follow Your Curiosities framework! You have the tools and insights to pay attention to your curiosities, harness the power of asking powerful questions to come up with creative solutions and ideas, and you have practiced how to take decisive action by choosing one small step to move forward with.

To continue to put these principles into practice, keep using the step-by-step worksheet to remain active on your curiosity journey with one small step at a time. This is just the start as you will undoubtedly encounter many more curiosities that you can apply this framework to in the future.

By adopting a curious mindset, asking powerful questions, and taking small steps toward your goals, you can unlock a world of possibilities to achieve your wildest flying pig dreams! And big dreams require small consistent actions. I encourage you to download a copy of the workbook which includes all the exercises from this book, and use it to remind yourself to take action whenever you encounter a curiosity that sparks your interest. With time and practice, you will become a master of curiosity, and you will fill your life with possibilities!

PART IV

CULTIVATING YOUR CURIOUS LIFE

"Whether you think you can, or you think you can't, you are right."

—Henry Ford

CHAPTER EIGHT

Mindset Matters

One of the key factors that separates those who accomplish their goals from those who don't is mindset. As you aspire toward your curiosities and define what success looks like for you, it's your mindset that's going to help or hinder you from bringing your ideas to life. Mindset is basically the lens or perspective through which we view the world and interpret events in our lives. It's this uniquely personal view of the world that shapes how we approach challenges, handle setbacks, and make decisions. It's a big deal because it influences how we navigate life.

I facilitate a workshop designed by Jimbo Clark called the B❒X Experience. The B❒X refers to the mindset box we each live in. Our boxes have served us in achieving our goals and creating possibilities—up to this point. Yet it has also limited us because our mindset boxes keep us safely in our comfort zone. In the B❒X Experience workshop, I help people not to think outside the box, rather as Jimbo puts it, "Build a better box." One where we are not limited by our past experiences, and one where we open up our lens to see from new and broader perspectives. Because when we expand our mindset, our thinking changes, and when we change the way we think, we can change our reality.

There are two types of mindsets most famously identified by Carol Dweck in her book, *Mindset*—fixed mindset and growth mindset. At one extreme, a fixed mindset is the belief that our abilities and qualities are set in stone and we can't change them. People with a fixed mindset tend to stick to what's known and comfortable, avoid challenges and risks, and fear judgment and failure. They believe that their intelligence, talents, and abilities are predetermined, and that there is little within their control that can be improved upon.

For example, a person with a fixed mindset who wants to start a business might think that they never could because they have never done it before. They believe they are unable to learn enough to figure out how to make it happen. They live in a limited mindset box.

On the other end of the scale, a growth mindset is the belief that our abilities and qualities can be developed. People with a growth mindset embrace challenges, persist in the face of setbacks, and value learning—believing that abilities and skills can develop with time and effort. They see failure as an opportunity to learn and grow, and they have confidence in their potential. They have built a better mindset box. When faced with the interest of starting a business, although they never have, they understand that they are capable of advancing their skills and abilities to reach their goal.

Most people don't fall strictly in the category of fixed or growth mindset. Many of us fall somewhere in between. It's a spectrum, and you might sit further to one side of the continuum than the other depending on the specific situation you find yourself in. The key is to recognize that mindset itself is not fixed, and a mindset toward growth can be cultivated and developed. By becoming aware of your own mindset tendencies and intentionally working toward a growth mindset, you can change the lens you see the world through and figuratively build yourself a better mindset box.

In my experience starting and running a business, I had to make a shift from a more fixed mindset to a growth mindset. Initially I often thought, "I can't start a business consultancy because I never have before, and I have no idea how." With the intention to shift my mindset toward growth, I realized I could change my perspective by adjusting my internal monologue and language. Rather than saying "I can't," I took on the habit of saying "I haven't yet," then figured out how to turn that "yet" into action steps. For example, "I haven't started a business serving corporate clients yet, but I can learn how." That simple shift in language allowed me to uncover new ideas, solve problems, and face challenges with the belief that I could learn how to overcome obstacles one small step at a time. I started taking classes on entrepreneurship. I became a certified Kaizen Muse Creativity Coach. I read books about business strategy and marketing, and I connected with people in similar fields from whom I could learn.

Instead of being held back by the limitations of a fixed mindset, I started seeing creative possibilities and opportunities for growth. Operating from a growth mindset, the impossible became possible.

Why does mindset matter when it comes to following your curiosity? Because your mindset powerfully impacts your behavior and ultimately determines the outcomes you achieve. If you have a fixed mindset, you're more likely to give up when things get tough, less likely to take risks, and it may stop you from even starting to pursue something new. But if you adopt a growth mindset, you're more likely to see your curiosity as potential, persevere through challenges, and take on new ideas and opportunities with enthusiasm. The quote by Henry Ford, "Whether you think you can, or you think you can't, you are right," highlights the power of our mindset and how it can govern our ability to achieve our goals. So think you can!

You might be wondering how to effectively shift your mindset across the continuum from fixed toward growth. There are a couple tools I want to share with you to directly confront fixed mindset and limiting beliefs, making space for you to move in the direction of your dreams and curiosities with more confidence, clarity, equipped with a growth mindset.

Operating from a growth mindset, the impossible becomes possible.

Reframe

The reframing tool is a powerful technique used to shift perspective in order to reinterpret situations or experiences in a more positive and empowering way—one that is not driven by our doubts and limiting beliefs. It involves consciously taking steps to change the way we think about a situation or event by considering alternate viewpoints.

When we reframe, we challenge our initial reactive thinking and seek more responsive and constructive meaning about a situation or circumstance. By using this process, we train our brains to be more optimistic, empowered, and growth-minded.

Here's how the reframing tool works, with an exercise to follow:

1. **Recognize your limiting belief.** Notice when you are experiencing a fixed mindset as your initial reaction to an event or new idea. This might sound like, "I can't," "I don't know how," or "This is a crazy idea." Then notice how this thought makes you feel and act.
2. **Challenge your initial reaction.** Question yourself and the validity of your initial interpretation. Oftentimes, you will find that it is rooted in a past experience or belief about yourself. Then ask yourself, "How might I view this situation in a different way?" One that is more positive, empowering, and constructive.
3. **Adopt a new frame of thought with evidence.** Once you have identified a more constructive interpretation of events, adopt this as your new frame of reference by citing evidence as to why this new way of thinking is possible.

Notice how your emotions have shifted from your initial limited thinking.

When you catch yourself thinking, "I can't do this," or "I'm not good enough," your brain is trying to keep you safe by avoiding a risk. Avert these limiting beliefs with the following activity.

Using the chart in your workbook, fill in the columns to shift your limiting beliefs. The columns from left to right are: Limiting Belief, New Belief, and Evidence. In the Limiting Belief column, write down your current negative or limiting thought, such as "I don't have the skills to write a book."

Then, in the New Belief column, reframe that thought into a positive and more empowering statement: "I can learn and find the resources needed to write a book."

Finally, in the Evidence column, provide evidence from your past to support your new belief, such as, "I have achieved what seemed to be impossible goals before, like when I learned to surf." Be as specific as you can with your evidence.

By reframing your thoughts in this way, you can overcome limiting beliefs and move toward success. Give it a try and see the positive impact it can have on your mindset, emotional well-being and movement toward turning your curiosities into possibilities.

LIMITING BELIEF	NEW BELIEF	EVIDENCE
ex. I DON'T KNOW HOW TO WRITE AND PUBLISH A BOOK.	I CAN FIND THE RESOURCES TO WRITE AND PUBLISH A BOOK.	I HAVE ACHIEVED WHAT SEEMED TO BE INSURMOUNTABLE GOALS BEFORE- LIKE WHEN I LEARNED TO SURF OR TRAVELED THROUGH EUROPE BY MYSELF.

Reframing is a valuable tool because it quickly helps us break free from the ruminations of negative and self-limiting fixed thinking patterns. It allows us to prove to ourselves with evidence that we are capable of growth and creating opportunities even in the face of challenges.

Appreciative Inquiry

Appreciative Inquiry is a problem-solving methodology that was developed in the 1980s by David Cooperrider and Suresh Srivastva in a doctoral program at Case Western Reserve University in Cleveland, Ohio. They observed that organizations typically used traditional problem-solving methods to overcome challenges. Methods which predominantly focus on identifying and fixing the immediate issue.

Cooperrider and Srivastva implemented a new approach that centered on helping organizations identify and exercise their strengths rather than focusing on the issue at hand. They called their approach Appreciative Inquiry. By identifying and utilizing strengths, organizations are able to repeatedly apply those assets to solve any challenge, not just the issue at hand.

The principles of Appreciative Inquiry for organizations can easily be applied to how we face challenges as well as new opportunities as individuals. Instead of dwelling on what's not working, explore your past successes and your personal strengths. Identify situations from your life where you have achieved your goals or prevailed over a hardship. What insights about your character and patterns of positive behavior can you find? These discoveries provide building blocks for you to replicate success.

When I think about my past achievements, a few of the strengths that come to mind are resilience, creative thinking, curiosity, and persistence. Knowing that those are characteristics that I have successfully used before, I can now deploy them like tools in a toolbox, applying them as needed to challenges, opportunities, and curiosities. Recognize your strengths, positive attributes, and past achievements. Utilize these truths to inspire yourself to pursue your "What if" and "How Might I" possibilities. You have the tools!

One of the first steps in the Appreciative Inquiry process is to identify your strengths. Take time for your personal appreciative inquiry deep dive to unearth the tools you carry around with you in the form of your strengths. Create a list or grounding rocks from your findings and refer to them as you face problems or feel stuck when pursuing a curiosity.

To uncover your strengths through an appreciative inquiry deep dive, creative exercises can be useful, such as the ones I share in my "Stronger Together by the Sum of Our Differences" workshop and keynote:

- Reflect on an accomplishment you are proud of and write down two to three traits or character strengths that helped you achieve it. For added creativity, build representations of your strengths with molding clay or LEGO® bricks.
- Select a hobby or talent and write it in the center of a blank piece of paper. Brainstorm all the character strengths you developed or utilized to become adept in that skill or talent.
- The Values in Action Institute on Character reports that knowing and applying your character strengths can increase happiness, boost confidence, reduce stress, and help you achieve your objectives. Take their Values in Action Character Strengths Survey, a free, research-based survey that will give insights into your top character strengths. (www.viacharacter.org)

Use the three prompts above to give yourself the advantage of knowing and utilizing your super powers as you follow your curiosities.

Surround Yourself with Support

During your curiosity journey, there will be moments of excitement when you feel like you could take on the world! Let's also acknowledge that bumps in the road are inevitable as you pursue those curiosities, and at times you may feel like your ideas are hopeless fantasies. In those moments, you can tap into the ideas and tools we talked about in this book to help you shift your mindset and reclaim your enthusiasm to keep moving forward toward your curiosity.

Another way to keep on track is by having the support of people who believe in you and possibly even your vision. I think it's important to distinguish that it's the belief in you that is essential, not necessarily in your idea. Of course, it would be wonderful if everyone thought your idea is pure genius, but who you really want in your corner are the people who believe that you can accomplish whatever you put your mind and effort to, regardless of the curiosity or idea you are in current pursuit of. These are the people you can rely on to "have your back," who offer honest advice and reactions. By building a network of supportive relationships, you can receive the encouragement, feedback, and resources you need to accomplish your goals.

You may or may not have this network of support in your life at this moment. Let's start by identifying who you have and who you need. I'm a firm believer in manifesting what you desire, starting by identifying what you want and need then writing it down. In this case, we're going to identify the type of support you need and see who in your life, or who you need to attract into your life to fill those roles. Identify these needs, then leave room to receive. There is no need to put pressure on yourself to actively search for these people. Be genuine in who you are, in what you are pursuing, take small action steps, and see who shows up in support of you. You'll be surprised, as it often happens in mysterious and serendipitous ways!

My Support System Activity

Make a list of three to five people in your life with whom you can share your big goals and small steps. Assign them specific roles in order to know exactly who to reach out to when you need that support:

- Encouragement/Emotional Support
- Accountability
- Resources

Determine what other support you might need and write those ideas down. Are there currently people in your life who could fill that gap? If yes, great! If no, then start talking to people about who and what you are looking for. Keep it as an active intention and watch who shows up!

I consider myself incredibly fortunate to have a support system of people who surround me with positive and limitless belief in me and my work. I also have to credit myself for creating an environment for those people to show up. I accomplished that using the tools in this book that I have shared with you. Tools like the act of wholeheartedly following my curiosity, uncovering and utilizing my strengths, and getting out of my comfort zone to make myself and my work visible.

When I first started my business, I joked that it wasn't growing steadily because nobody knew about it except my mom and a few friends. And there was truth to that. I wasn't making enough noise, meeting enough people, or courageously asking for the help

I needed. Once I was able to get past the avoidance of cold outreach, posting on LinkedIn, and asking for help—I was able to attract people into my corner who, without hesitation, became my encouragement, support system, accountability partners, resources, collaborators, and friends.

I encourage you to do the same. Make yourself, your curiosities, and your needs visible. It will be uncomfortable at first, but as we know—discomfort is where growth lives. The more practice you give this, and the more of yourself you put into it, the easier it becomes as your confidence grows.

When I decided to make my work more visible, I received advice from my friend and Collaboration Coach, Baily Hancock, to post more on LinkedIn. Specifically, she suggested creating and posting short videos where I talk about the work I do. She also advised me to create a post asking for referrals for podcast appearances. Although I sat in that meeting nodding at everything she said, the voice in my head was screaming, 'There is no way I'm doing any of this. Ever.' If we are connected on LinkedIn, you know that I overcame that resistance. I now prolifically and enthusiastically use that platform to drive visibility. Doing so has opened up a world of possibilities for me, including the growth of my company and, most importantly—introducing me to wonderful people. If this stubborn, self-reliant introvert can do it, you can too!

CHAPTER NINE

Pigs *Can* Fly!

Curiosity is the whisper of ideas that sparks our imagination, encouraging us to do things differently, fueling us to move forward toward new possibilities. At its core, curiosity asks us to be open-minded, to embrace the unknown, and to tap into our imagination. It challenges us to get out of our comfort zone and conventional ways of thinking. When we learn to pause to pay attention to our curiosities, we can start asking questions that are creative and expansive like, "Why?", "How?", and "What if?", which then leads us to creative solutions and possibilities we may not have come up with before.

Remember to employ the tools of pausing, wondering, and wandering to pay attention to those curiosities that tap you on the shoulder. Ask powerful questions that start with "what if" and "how might I" to explore creative ways to move forward with your curiosity. Then start by taking just one small step in the direction of those curiosities.

As we come to the end of our journey together, I hope you feel excited for what's ahead. Your curiosities are waiting for you to pay attention to them. They are ideas asking for you to give them consideration and life, one small step at a time. You don't have to have all the answers or know exactly how you'll get from here to there. Just keep following your curiosity, take one step at a time, and trust that the path will unfold for you.

I believe in our curiosities because I saw what it allowed my refugee parents to create for their family out of the necessity of following curiosity when there was no other choice. Their path reminds me of this excerpt from Brianna Wiest's book, *The Pivot Year*—"Nobody is brave at the beginning. Bravery is dug out of the deepest part of us, often by necessity. It happens when you allow your love for something to grow a little larger than your fear of it." Allow your love for your curiosities and the possibilities they hold grow larger than your fears.

Through the sacrifices and example of my parents, I now get to follow and even chase my curiosities, not from necessity, purely because, I can. What a privilege. A privilege you have too. Let's individually and collectively follow our curiosities. Together we can create a world where pigs *can* fly.

Keep dreaming big and taking small steps toward your curiosities. I once co-facilitated a LEGO® SERIOUS PLAY® methods training at NASA's Jet Propulsion Laboratory. On the wall read their motto, "Dare Mighty Things." Thank you for joining me on this journey. I wish you the most wonderful adventures, joyful challenges, and personal growth as you follow your curiosities, discover new possibilities, and dare mighty things.

DARE
MIGHTY
THINGS

Curiosity is the most powerful thing you own.

I hope you have enjoyed this journey. The next time you find yourself curious about something, I wonder what possibilities you could create for yourself and others, if you follow that curiosity with 'What if', and you follow that 'What if', with the courage to take one small step forward.

Van

#whatifpigscanfly
worksmartadvantage.com/whatifpigscanfly
Watch my TEDx Talk, What If? The Life Changing Power of Curiosity and Courage

ABOUT THE AUTHOR

Van Lai-DuMone is the founder of worksmart Advantage, where she actively works to rewrite the way we apply creativity in the workplace, instilling brave thinking in clients who are willing to disrupt traditional learning and development methods.

Van proposes that we are all innately curious and creative, therefore good ideas can come from any level of an organization. And by cultivating idea-sharing in the workplace, everyone has a chance to have their voice heard. And when that happens—company culture, performance, and innovation can skyrocket!

Van brings over 20 years of corporate and start-up experience into designing and implementing learning and development programs for her clients–using her proprietary Creative Integration™ strategies. Van serves as a fractional learning officer to mid-sized high growth organizations curious about developing a creative learning culture. She studied psychology at the University of California, Santa Barbara and earned her MBA from Pepperdine University. Watch her TEDx Talk titled What if? The Life Changing Power of Curiosity and Courage!

Van has a son and three dogs. Currently, she is letting her curiosity find her a way to living on a farm with miniature highland cows and a workshop to create stained-glass art. Stay tuned!

CONNECT WITH VAN

Van Lai-DuMone is available for speaking, workshops, and interviews.

- Website: www.worksmartadvantage.com
- Email: van@worksmartadvantage.com
- LinkedIn @Van Lai-DuMone
- Instagram @worksmartadvantage

worksmart Advantage is a progressive team and leadership development company that works with organizations to transform co-workers into teammates and managers into leaders through Creative Integration™ - the use of creativity, play, and shared experiences as primary learning methodologies. Don't be surprised when you see a DJ, spoken word artist, or a stack of LEGO® bricks in front of you at one of our programs.

We integrate creative thinking and creative problem solving into learning and development to transform your company into a place where innovation is abundant, people thrive, and your business skyrockets!

Learn more at worksmartadvantage.com

ABOUT THE ILLUSTRATOR

Sarah Moyle is an illustrator, creative facilitator, speaker, and Chief Play Officer at Intel Corporation. Since architecting her own unique role shortly after joining the company in 2011, Sarah has been a champion of play, creativity, and visual thinking at Intel and beyond. She is passionate about reigniting and fostering the innate creativity and playfulness in everyone she works with to have hard fun and unlock innovative ideas. When she isn't playing at Intel, Sarah delights in getting outdoors with her two children, spending time with friends, crafting, and making spooky plans for her elaborate Halloween display each year!

CONNECT WITH SARAH

Sarah Moyle is available for illustration, speaking, workshops, and interviews.

- Website: www.sarahmoyle.com
- Email: sarah.d.moyle@gmail.com
- LinkedIn @Sarah Moyle
- Instagram @Sarahmoyledraws

What if Pigs *Can* Fly?

A Practical Workbook
to Follow Your Curiosities
to Achieve Impractical Possibilities

www.worksmartadvantage.com/whatifpigscanfly

Curiosity

:noun

- a desire to know or discover
- an interest leading to inquiry ... and possibility!

:might sound like

- "What if...?"
- "I wonder ..."

Use this workbook to experience the Follow Your Curiosity Framework!

Download additional copies at:
www.worksmartadvantage.com/whatifpigscanfly

As a child, how did you respond to curiosities? How has that changed in adulthood?

For many of us adults, we have lost our innate ability to follow our curiosities. This workbook gives you tools to get back to that childhood wonder and take action on your curiosities!

A Framework

to follow your curiosities

Step 1. Uncover your curiosities.
Step 2. Explore by asking powerful questions.
Step 3. Take one small step.

How far has curiosity already taken you?
Use the space below:

1. In the left-hand column, jot down some of your accomplishments.
2. In the right-hand column, identify the initial curiosity that led you there.

ACCOMPLISHMENT	CURIOSITY

Through this exercise, how can you see that curiosity has already created possibilities for you?

Benefits
of curiosity

- Enhanced creativity: Curiosity inspires us to think outside the box and come up with novel ideas and approaches to challenges and opportunities.
- Improved problem-solving skills: When we are curious, we are more likely to explore multiple solutions to a problem rather than settling for the first one that comes to mind.
- Increased adaptability: Curiosity allows us to be more open to change and new experiences, which can help us adapt more easily to a variety of situations.
- Greater happiness and fulfillment: Curiosity can bring a sense of excitement and purpose to life as we pursue our natural interests.

Add your own thoughts:

Step 1.

Uncover Your Curiosities

Brainstorm

your curiosities

Brainstorm your interests and things that spark your curiosity. Use the prompts below to guide your brainstorming. Pick a couple of the bullet pointed ideas to bring some creativity to this exercise:

- Rather than writing your ideas in a linear fashion, draw clouds on a piece of blank white paper and fill those clouds in with your curiosities.
- Use markers rather than a pen or pencil.
- Sketch your answers.
- Grab magazines, a pair of scissors, and a glue stick and collage your answers.
- Interview yourself-or ask people who know you well enough to answer these questions about you.

Prompts:

1. What topics or activities do you enjoy reading or learning?
2. What are some questions that keep coming back to you?
3. What life experiences have sparked your curiosity?
4. What hobbies or interests have you always wanted to pursue but have not had the chance to?
5. If you had unlimited time and resources, what would you explore or learn more about?

Start exploring your curiosities on the next page.

My Curiosities

They may sound like ...

- 'I wonder ...'
- 'I've always wanted to ...'
- 'If I could I would ...'
- 'Wouldn't it be fun to ...'

They may look like ...

- A persistent interest
- A childhood dream
- An unexplored talent
- Something you want to try

Divergent Thinking

Divergent thinking is the process of generating as many ideas as possible without evaluation. Practice divergent thinking with this exercise.

Below you see an image of a clothing iron. Ask yourself, 'What is this used for?' Your first response will most likely be, 'Ironing clothes.' Now ask yourself, 'What else?' and let your imagination run wild. Remember the hallmarks of divergent thinking are that all ideas make it to the table, there is no judgment or criteria, and seek quantity over quality. Come up with as many uses for this iron as you can.

Step 2.

Explore By Asking Powerful Questions

Practice Powerful Questions

like 'What if?' and 'How might I?'

Now that you have identified some current curiosities. Pick one to practice asking powerful questions about by writing it down in the center of a blank sheet of paper and circle it. Then start asking powerful question about your curiosity. Your answers could take the form of statements like:

- I might ...
- I could ...
- It would be fun to ...

As a reminder, here's my example. Then use the next page to create yours!

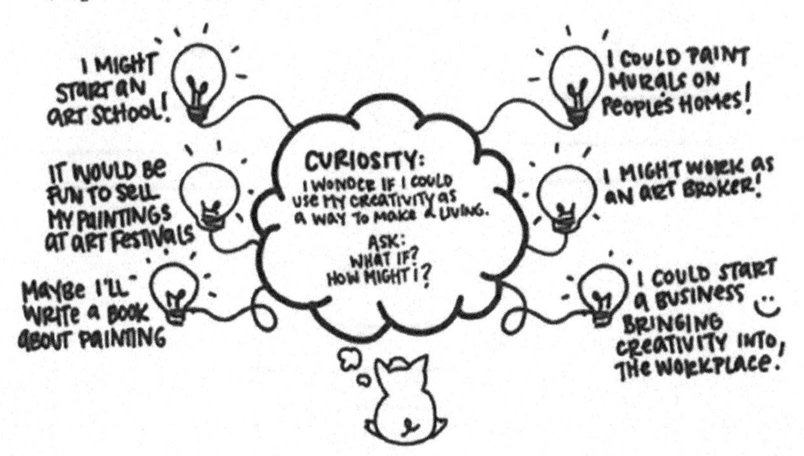

Your turn!
Remember to apply ...

DIVERGENT THINKING

PROCESS OF COMING UP WITH AS MANY IDEAS AS POSSIBLE

Step 3.

Take One Small Step.

Narrow Down.

Now that you have come up with divergent ideas about how you might move forward with your curiosity, Let's narrow down to one idea and one small step to move forward with by filtering your 'I might' statements through the convergent thinking process.

Look at your 'I might,' 'I could,' and 'It would be fun if' statements from the last exercise.

Follow these steps to filter your ideas through a set of criteria in order to narrow down and identify the idea you want to move forward with - from there, we will create your first small step.

Step 1. Set your parameters. Write down three to four statements to filter your ideas through.

1. ______________________________

2. ______________________________

3. ______________________________

4. ______________________________

Step 2. Filter each of your 'I might' statements through those parameters and see which ones are able to make it across. We'll call these your 'light bulb' ideas.

Apply convergent thinking to identify your 'light bulb' ideas and move those ideas to the right side of the arrows.

Step 3. Filter to one idea. If you still have more than one, pick the one idea that excites you the most to move forward with.

One Small Step.

Congratulations! You have identified the one idea you want to move forward with. Let's find one small step to get you started.

To find that small step toward your narrowed down idea, go through the divergent and convergent exercises again:

Step 1. Using divergent thinking, brainstorm ideas regarding one small step you can take toward achieving your converged idea. Come up with as many small steps as you can to give yourself options. Recall that the characteristics of divergent thinking include: all ideas make it to the table, no judgment of ideas, and welcome wild and crazy ideas!

You can write them in on the steps below:

Step 2. Once you are done ideating, move to convergent thinking, which entails setting your criteria for filtering your small step ideas down to two or three that meet the standards of your criteria.

My Small Step Criteria: .

1. ______________________________

2. ______________________________

3. ______________________________

4. ______________________________

Narrowing Down My Small Step:

My One Small Step.

Pick one small step to start with, and write it down below. Remember, there is no such thing as a step that is too small. Make sure your small step is small enough that you will take action.

Accountability.
Hold yourself accountable by filling in the blanks below:

I will ___________________________, by ________.

(insert small step)

(insert timeframe < 48 hours away)

Track Your Small Steps.

Yay! You have identified your first small step, use this worksheet to begin your curiosity journey starting with that one small step. Write out subsequent steps as they come to you, reaching your goal by climbing one small step at a time.

TRACK YOUR SMALL STEPS

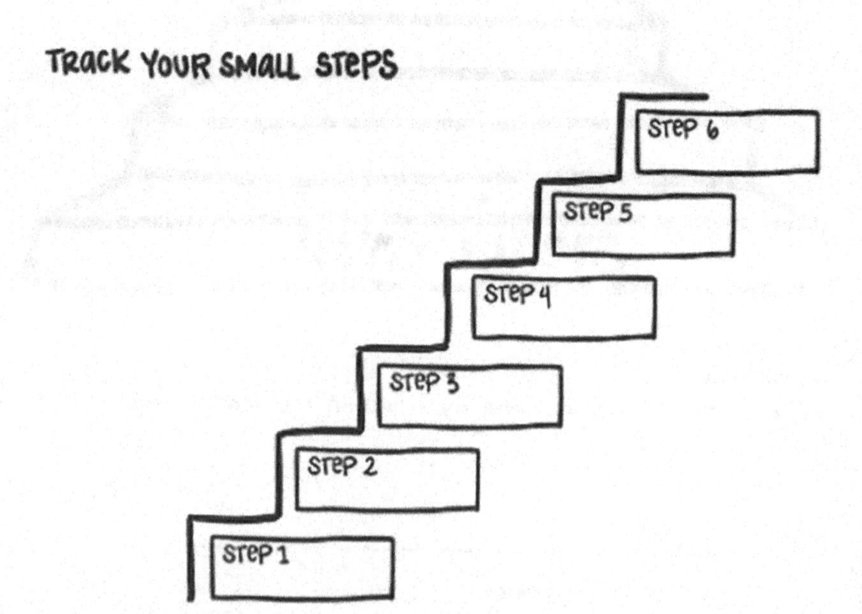

Mindset Matters.

Cultivate a Curious Life.

Reframe

your limiting beliefs

When we reframe, we challenge our initial reactive thinking and seek more responsive and constructive meaning about a situation or circumstance. By using this process, we train our brains to be more optimistic, empowered, and growth-minded.

Here's how the reframing tool works, with an exercise to follow:

1. Recognize your limiting belief. Notice when you are experiencing a fixed mindset as your initial reaction to an event or new idea. This might sound like, "I can't," "I don't know how," or 'This is a crazy idea.' Then notice how this thought makes you feel and act.

2. Challenge your initial reaction. Question yourself and the validity of your initial interpretation. Oftentimes, you will find that it is rooted in a past experience or belief about yourself. Then ask yourself, "How might I view this situation in a different way?" One that is more positive, empowering, and constructive.

3. Adopt a new frame of thought with evidence. Once you have identified a more constructive interpretation of events, adopt this as your new frame of reference by citing evidence as to why this new frame of thinking is possible. Notice how your emotions have shifted from your initial limited thinking.

Use the worksheet on the next page to practice reframing limiting beliefs.

Reframing Tool

LIMITING BELIEF	NEW BELIEF	EVIDENCE
ex. I DON'T KNOW HOW TO WRITE AND PUBLISH A BOOK.	I CAN FIND THE RESOURCES TO WRITE AND PUBLISH A BOOK.	I HAVE ACHIEVED WHAT SEEMED TO BE INSURMOUNTABLE GOALS BEFORE- LIKE WHEN I LEARNED TO SURF OR TRAVELED THROUGH EUROPE BY MYSELF.

Reframing is a valuable tool because it quickly helps us break free from the ruminations of negative and self-limiting fixed thinking patterns. It allows us to prove to ourselves with evidence that we are capable of growth and creating opportunities even in the face of challenges.

Appreciative Inquiry

Take time to do your personal appreciative inquiry deep dive, and identify the tools you carry around with you in the form of your strengths. Create a list or some grounding rocks from your findings and refer to them as you face problems or feel stuck when pursuing a curiosity.

Reflect on an accomplishment you are proud of and write down two to three traits or character strengths that helped you achieve it. For added creativity, sketch or build representations of your strengths with molding clay or LEGO® bricks.

My Support System

Make sure to surround yourself with support. By building a network of supportive relationships, you can receive the encouragement, feedback, and resources you need to accomplish your goals.

Make a list of three to five people in your life with whom you can share your big goals and small steps, and assign them specific roles so you know exactly who to reach out to when you need some support.

NAME	ROLE
1. ____________________	____________________
2. ____________________	____________________
3. ____________________	____________________
4. ____________________	____________________

Determine what other support you might need and write those ideas down. Are there currently people in your life who could fill that gap? If yes, great! If no, then start talking to people about who and what you are looking for. Keep it as an active intention and watch who shows up!

____________________ ____________________

____________________ ____________________

The End.

or The Beginning

What If Pigs Can Fly?
www.worksmartadvantage.com/whatifpigscanfly